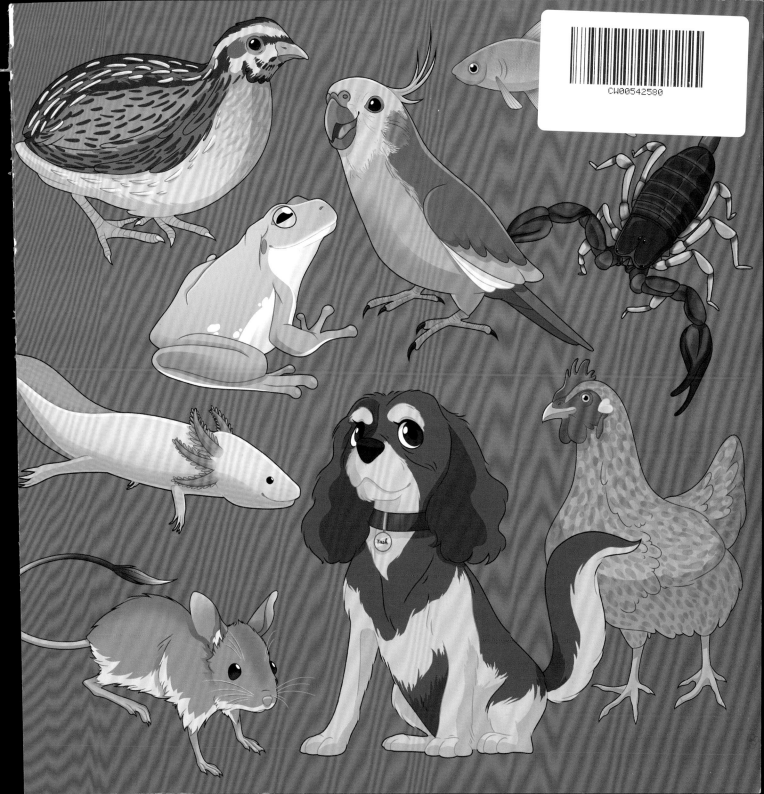

# THE ULTIMATE PET HANDBOOK

## AN ESSENTIAL GUIDE FOR YOUNG PEOPLE WITH A PASSION FOR PETS

• • • • • • • • • • • • • •

### BY BEN DESSEN

### ILLUSTRATED BY NIKKITA ARCHER

For Mum and Dad.
Thank you for allowing me to grow up in a home full of pets to love and for encouraging me to live my dreams.

To all my pets over the years, thank you for being my inspiration in life and teaching me so much.

# FOREWORD

. . . . . . . . . . . .

## BY DR HARRY COOPER BVSC OAM

As you read this book it will soon be obvious that Ben Dessen is no ordinary
individual. From a very young age Ben has had a fascination with animals of all kinds.
He has the greatest enthusiasm for the conservation of not only Australian wildlife,
but for many other species that find themselves close to extinction.

Ben travels widely to see first-hand how different animals are surviving in the world.
He is active on social media, making it easy to keep up with him and his adventures.
Ben has been involved in the plight of the orangutan in Borneo; clearing their
rainforest habitat to plant millions of oil palm trees is leaving orangutans without
a home. Like so many of our beautiful animals, their very survival is dependent on
maintaining the environment in which they live.

Ben is a manager of one of the most modern and diverse pet stores in Australia.
His knowledge of reptiles in particular, is amazing. If you are keen on snakes or lizards,
then he has the answers. Ben's strong belief is, the more we can learn about the
creatures we share our planet with, the more we can learn about ourselves and how
to better protect the environment for the future.

You may have seen Ben on morning television, where he chats about different animals, with extensive knowledge and obvious affection. You can also find Ben giving talks to various organisations and he is always willing to help with advice if you are having a problem with your more 'unusual' pet.

What about the man himself? Well I have known Ben for a very long time. I have watched him grow from a young bloke who was keen on anything that was alive, into a man with great communication skills, amazing knowledge and unrelenting drive. Ben is always a pleasure to talk with and has all the tools necessary to make a great impact in the world of animals. He could even be another David Attenborough!

Ben amazes me with his tireless energy, his continual smile and his determination. Above all else I am proud to call Ben Dessen my friend.

# WORDS FROM BOB IRWIN

It is very important for children to not only learn about cuddly pets, but also about some of the creatures in the environment that are not always recognised as being important. Ben Dessen is one of the most passionate and knowledgeable of his generation of animal enthusiasts. Listen very carefully to what Ben has to say about taking responsibility for all animals and the environment.

*— Bob Irwin*
*(father of Steve Irwin)*

# CONTENTS

• • • • • • • • • • • • • • • • • • • • •

## Furry Pets – Mammals

## Scaly Pets – Reptiles

## Creepy Crawly Pets – Critters

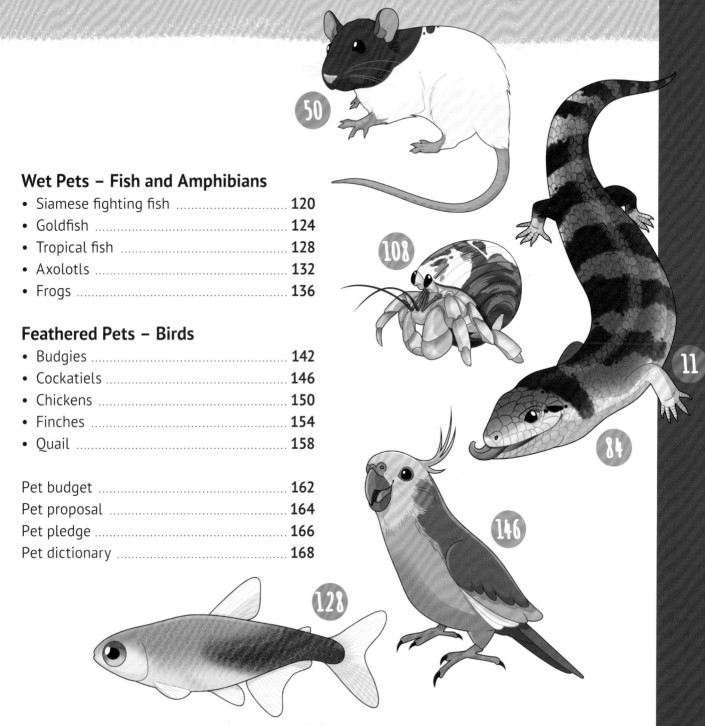

50

108

11

84

146

128

# MY ANIMAL OBSESSION

I've always loved animals. From the tiniest ant, to the largest whale in the ocean, I can't remember a time when everything about living creatures and dinosaurs didn't fascinate me. My defining childhood memory was when my parents surprised me with a pet snake for my sixth birthday. From that moment, I was completely obsessed. No bigger than a worm, that gorgeous little children's python captured my heart and set me on my path in life. I knew then, as I know now, all I ever want to do is surround myself with animals.

I was very lucky to grow up living on a bush block in suburban Sydney with wildlife literally on my doorstep. I spent every spare second exploring: collecting cicada shells, catching yabbies in the creek and spotting powerful owls in the treetops. Our home was filled with creatures too. From budgies to bearded dragons, stick insects to fighting fish, and pythons large and small. I even had a pet eel named Elvis who I rescued from the local fish market.

I learned early in life that kids can make a big difference by helping animals in need. After getting off the school bus one afternoon, I came across an injured brush-tailed possum unable to climb. I gently scooped her up in my jumper and carried her home. The vet later discovered 'Duchess' had multiple gunshot wounds from a pellet gun. I couldn't believe people could be so cruel. I was beyond happy when Duchess – and the baby later found in her pouch – could be saved and eventually released.

Animals filled my days and my dreams for the future. As I got older, I continued bringing pets into my life and protecting native animals, becoming a member of our local wildlife rescue organisation. In high school, I studied anything animal related and worked weekends with farm animals before moving on to join the largest pet store in Australia. Caring for animals is my greatest passion and an incredible privilege I try to never take for granted.

After leaving school I continued to build my knowledge by gaining a degree in animal science and travelling the world to see all sorts of animals in the wild. In 2011 I volunteered in Borneo where I worked with a group of young people to set up a new orangutan rehabilitation centre. Helping to

## I WAS BEYOND HAPPY WHEN DUCHESS — AND THE BABY LATER FOUND IN HER POUCH — COULD BE SAVED AND EVENTUALLY RELEASED.

• • • • • • • • • • • • • • • • • • • •

save a three-year-old orangutan, Jojo, will always be one of the greatest highlights of my life. Catching crocs in Cape York with Bob Irwin was another unforgettable adventure.

I continue to live and work with pets and wildlife. I take every opportunity to educate others about the amazing animals we share this planet with. Animals teach me many

things; perhaps, most importantly, how we are all connected. Every living creature has a role in the natural environment we depend upon for survival. Animals deserve our respect and need our protection. In return they reward us with the joy and love they bring to our lives.

By sharing my experience with pets, I hope this book inspires you to become an animal ambassador for all creatures and take the Pet Pledge. By taking the pledge you promise to be a responsible pet carer and to do your very best to protect all animals and our precious environment.

Enjoy, Ben.

# PLANNING FOR A PET

## WELCOME TO THE AMAZING WORLD OF PETS!

. . . . . . . . . . . . . . . . . . . . . .

Humans have always shared their lives with animals. Pets make great companions and loyal friends. They love and accept us just the way we are. Growing up with pets teaches us how to be more gentle, patient and kinder to others. Opening our homes and hearts to pets can also help us care more about wildlife and the environment.

Bringing a pet into your life can be the best experience ever, but it is one you need to take very seriously and carefully plan for. Whether you're looking to get your first pet, or you're an animal lover like me, thinking about getting your next pet, this book is the ultimate tool for you. You'll find everything you need to plan the perfect Pet Proposal to pitch to the adults in your life. Learn about awesome animals for you and your family to love in the Pet Profiles. By understanding what an animal needs, you'll be able to give your special friend a safe, happy and healthy life.

### LIFE IS BETTER WITH PETS.

. . . . . . . . .

# BEING A RESPONSIBLE PET CARER

Choosing to bring a pet into your life is a huge responsibility. Like us, many animals are sentient beings, meaning they experience feelings such as sadness, stress and joy. This means caring for a pet involves a lot more than just giving an animal food, water and shelter.

Pets need enrichment (stimulation) and love to live their best lives. Animals in your care depend on you for survival. You must be ready and capable of fully committing to your animal for its entire life.

Some people buy pets for the wrong reasons. They might think it's 'cool', maybe they want to surprise a friend with a pet as a gift, or they just fall in love with that cute baby animal in the pet store. Making an impulse pet purchase for yourself or someone else is a very bad decision. Sadly, such pets often don't receive the attention they need and deserve, or worse, they are neglected.

Being a responsible pet carer means making informed choices with animal welfare as your main priority.

# CHOOSING THE RIGHT PET

With so many fascinating and unique animals, how do you decide which pet is best for you?

My advice is to always let the animal's needs guide your choice. By meeting their needs, you will ensure your pet thrives and this will bring you great happiness.

Of course, your own needs are also important. Caring for a pet is a two-way relationship. You may have an interest in a certain type of animal (mammal, reptile, insect, fish, amphibian, bird). You may prefer an interactive (hands-on) or an observational (hands-off) animal. But ultimately, your pet's needs must come before your own desire for an animal.

ALL ANIMALS NEED YOU TO DEVOTE TIME TO THEIR CARE.
· · · · · · · ·

HEALTHY BIRD'S
Budgie Seed

Providing the best life for any pet, means trying to recreate the most natural home environment for each species. As you read the Pet Profiles to find your favourite animal friend ask yourself the following three key questions:

# ① HOW MUCH SPACE DO I HAVE AVAILABLE?
· · · · · · · · · · · · · · · · · · · · · · · · · · · · · ·

Some pets, such as dogs, rabbits, guinea pigs, chickens and birds need plenty of space for exercise. If you have a small backyard, or no backyard, it will be harder to meet the enrichment (stimulation) needs of these animals. On the other hand, there are many animals (reptiles, fish, insects, rats and mice) whose needs can be more easily met with smaller enclosures or aquariums. These animals can be kept indoors and don't take up much space at all.

## 2 HOW MUCH TIME CAN I REGULARLY COMMIT TO MY PET?

All animals need you to devote time to their care. The amount of time you need to give and what you will need to do (feed, clean, interact, exercise) will vary and depend on the species and number of pets you commit to. Some pets (snakes, insects) require very little time as they need less frequent feeding, cleaning and interaction. Many pets (dogs, cats, rabbits, birds, rats and mice) require a lot more of your time and loving interaction each day.

## 3 WHAT SUPPORT DO I HAVE?

Getting help from the adults in your life to make your pet dream a reality is very important. While some pets (insects, fighting fish) can be less expensive to set up and maintain, other pets (reptiles, amphibians) can be much more expensive. Some pets (dogs, cats) will also need to see the vet each year. You will need adult support to set up and meet ongoing pet-care expenses for the life of your animal. Why not make it a team effort and share the fun of bonding with your pet with the whole family to get the assistance you need.

17

# BEYOND DOGS AND CATS – ALTERNATIVE PETS

When most people think of a pet the animals that usually come to mind are dogs and cats. Dogs and cats make great pets. In fact, humans first domesticated dogs over 15,000 years ago, making them one of our first pets. These days, many people live in apartments, have busy jobs, or attend schools that take them away from home for long hours. This can make it difficult, or impossible, to give a dog or cat all the space, time and love that they need.

Changing lifestyles have led to a huge increase in the popularity of alternative pets. Today, many different types of animals are kept as pets. While not all these animals enjoy a tummy rub like a dog, or curling up for a cuddle like a cat, they do offer their own unique characters and can be very rewarding creatures to share your life with.

So, what creatures make suitable alternative pet options? For animal lovers like you and me, snakes, lizards, frogs and insects can make fascinating companions.

### SNAKES, LIZARDS, FROGS AND INSECTS CAN MAKE FASCINATING COMPANIONS.

• • • • • • • • • • • • • • • • • •

These animals do not require much space, do not bark, scratch the furniture, or shed hair. Some don't even need to be fed every day. By caring for these gorgeous creatures, we can also try to help others appreciate them and begin to change negative attitudes towards snakes and other creepy crawlies.

The Pet Profiles will help you learn about many awesome alternative pet choices.

-PLANNING FOR A PET-

# CONVINCING THE ADULTS

One of the major roadblocks to getting a pet is often convincing the adults in your life to support you. I was very lucky to have parents who encouraged my passion to care for all kinds of animals. I made sure they didn't need to nag me to feed and clean enclosures because I enjoyed spending time with my animals. I would never have been allowed to bring so many pets into our lives if I didn't love and care for them well.

I know many adults are not as open to the idea of having pets in the house as mine were. This is exactly why I have some helpful tips for convincing the adults in your life that pets can be a great addition to your family.

# NUMBER ONE TIP: SHOW YOUR COMMITMENT AND MEAN IT

By far, the most important thing you can do to convince the adults in your life you are ready to accept the responsibility of caring for a pet is to show them how committed you are.

Use the Pet Profiles to choose the animal you know you can care for best and love the most. Complete a Pet Budget using the checklist for your chosen pet to make sure you plan for everything they need. If you have a well-prepared Pet Proposal to pitch, they're more likely to support your dream of getting a pet.

Adults tend to have a number of common objections to getting a pet, and you might want to include some of the following ideas in the Pet Proposal you will soon be pitching to them.

## 'YOU WILL JUST GET BORED WITH IT AND WE WILL END UP LOOKING AFTER IT.'

If you have a bad track record for losing interest in past hobbies this could be a hard argument to win in the short term. You will need to prove yourself. Borrow books about the pet you would like to care for from the library. Read as much as you can. You can never be too prepared and this will show how serious you are. Give the adults in your life time to see you are not losing interest. Every month bring up the pet topic again by sharing something new you have discovered about the animal.

The enclosures of some pets (mice, rats, rabbits and chickens) will get messy and smell if they are not cleaned regularly. If you are interested in caring for one of these animals, you will need to spend some time cleaning every day. Sticking to this promise is not only very important for your animal's health and hygiene (cleanliness), but also to show respect for the opportunity you have been given. Other pets (reptiles, insects, fish and amphibians) are less messy and their enclosures don't need to be cleaned as often. If mess and smells are the main objection to keeping a pet in your home, perhaps choosing one of these animals to love may suit your family situation better.

## 'PETS ARE MESSY AND SMELLY.'

## 'WE DON'T HAVE SPACE FOR A PET.'

If you only have a small outdoor area, or limited space inside the house, choose a pet that doesn't take up much room. Some pets (reptiles, fish, insects, rats, mice and amphibians) can easily be kept in your bedroom. Show the adults in your life the exact amount of space your animal will need and where they could happily live in your home.

## 'PETS ARE TOO EXPENSIVE.'

The cost to purchase and provide for all the needs of different animals varies. Some animals (stick insects, Siamese fighting fish, mice and rats) are much less expensive to care for than others (dogs, cats and reptiles). You will need to prepare a Pet Budget to show the set-up and ongoing costs for your chosen pet. Offer to contribute your savings or do extra jobs around the house to help pay for what your animal will need.

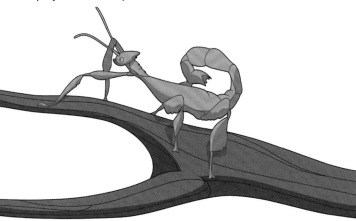

## 'WHAT HAPPENS WHEN WE WANT TO GO ON HOLIDAYS?'

Ask your relatives or close friends and their parents if they would be willing to care for your pet if you go away on holidays and can't take your animal with you (maybe offer to do the same for them). If this isn't an option for you, see if there is a reliable pet sitter in your area and find out how much they would cost. This will show the adults in your life you are thinking ahead and taking responsibility for your animal.

Snakes are the pets that meet the most resistance from adults. Many people fear snakes. Try taking them to a good pet store with reptiles, or a zoo, where they can meet one up-close. Speak with expert snake-loving staff to clear up any misconceptions. Who knows, they might even end up holding a snake and discovering what incredible animals they are.

'I'M SCARED OF SNAKES AND DON'T WANT ONE IN THE HOUSE.'

'WE DON'T WANT MICE AND RATS IN THE FREEZER.'

The thought of having mice and rats in the freezer to feed a snake is enough to freak out most parents. We had a 'reptile food drawer' in our freezer when I was growing up. All the snake food was kept on its own, in clearly labelled, sealed plastic containers. Reassure your adults they won't need to see or touch anything gross.

# MAKING A BUDGET

Part of being a responsible pet carer means being able to provide for everything your animal needs to live a healthy and happy life. The least expensive aspect of caring for a pet, is the pet itself. Preparing a Pet Budget will help you think about all the costs involved.

After reading the Pet Profiles and choosing an animal, use the checklist to write down all the things they need on a Pet Budget form. Visit your local pet shop or do an online search to find out the cost of each item on your list. You may need an adult to help you do this, but be prepared by knowing what you are looking for.

## PET BUDGET

You will find a blank Pet Budget form to copy at the back of this book. Here is one I have filled out as an example to show you how easy it is to do.

24

# PET BUDGET

| SET UP COSTS | TYPE OF PET | Pygmy Bearded Dragon |
|---|---|---|
| **COST/ADOPTION FEE OF ANIMAL** | | $100 |
| **HOUSING & EQUIPMENT** | | |
| Enclosure | | $250 |
| Day basking globe and fitting | | $45 |
| UVB globe and fitting | | $80 |
| Thermostat | | $150 |
| Basking log | | $50 |
| Food and water bowls | | $25 |
| Artificial plants | | $40 |
| Substrate | | $30 |
| Calcium and vitamin powder | | $20 |
| Reptile disinfectant | | $25 |
| **SET UP TOTAL** | | **$815** |

## ONGOING COSTS

| | Pygmy Bearded Dragon |
|---|---|
| **FOOD** | |
| Live insects | $10 (weekly)= $520 (yearly) |
| Fruits and vegetables | $5 (weekly)= $260 (yearly) |
| Lizard pellets | $20 (bi-monthly) = $120 (yearly) |
| **MAINTENANCE** | |
| Replace substrate | $30 (every 4 months) =$90 (yearly) |
| Replace heat light | $15 (when it blows) = $60 (yearly) |
| Replace UVB globe | $50 (yearly) |
| **VET CARE** | None required for bearded dragons |
| **ONGOING COSTS TOTAL (Yearly)** | **$1100** |

# WHERE TO FIND A PET

You can find an animal to love in many places. Unfortunately, not all people treat animals with the care and respect they deserve. It is very important to source your pet from the right place. First, consider adopting a pet from a rescue shelter. Private breeders and pet stores can also be good options. You can often get helpful recommendations about where to find your pet from animal societies, clubs and interest groups.

## ADOPTION

Some animals are surrendered or abandoned because people are unable or unwilling to continue to care for them. These animals often find themselves in a rescue shelter. Giving these animals a second chance at life in a loving home through adoption is a wonderful place to start your search for a new pet.

There are many rescue organisations that do fantastic work helping all sorts of animals. You will need an adult to help you contact these places to see if there is a suitable animal for your family to offer a forever home to.

## PRIVATE BREEDERS

Some people breed and sell animals from their own homes. You may see advertisements for their animals online. If you are considering purchasing a pet from a breeder, always take an adult with you to inspect their facilities. Make sure their animals look healthy and well cared for. Good breeders love their animals and will be very knowledgeable and selective about who they let them go home with.

## PET STORES

Pet stores can be great places to find an animal, its enclosure, accessories and food all in one place. Good pet stores take great care of their animals. Check to see if the animals on display look healthy and their enclosures are clean and well maintained.

Better pet stores will have highly trained staff willing to spend time answering all your questions. In fact, their staff may not allow you to purchase an animal if they're not convinced you can care for it properly. The best pet stores will guarantee the health of their animals and be willing to support you and your pet long after you leave the store.

## ANIMAL SOCIETIES, CLUBS AND INTEREST GROUPS

Some animal lovers form societies, clubs and interest groups to share their passion for specific pets. There are budgie clubs, fish and reptile societies, guinea pig, rabbit and rodent groups, just to name a few. Consider joining one and networking with other young pet lovers and experts to get their recommendations of ethical (high standards) places to find your special pet.

Whether you choose to adopt or source your pet privately, you will usually still need to visit a pet store for housing, accessories and food for your animal. Before you bring your new pet home, make sure you have everything set up ready and waiting to welcome them. This will reduce the stress on you and your animal so you can relax and enjoy this special time.

**BEFORE YOU BRING YOUR NEW PET HOME, MAKE SURE YOU HAVE EVERYTHING SET UP READY AND WAITING TO WELCOME THEM.**

ADOPT AUSTRALIA

SEARCH

# ANIMAL REGISTRATION AND LICENSING

In Australia, there are different laws protecting animals in each state and territory. It can be confusing with a range of registration and licensing rules across the country.

The cost of registration (dogs and cats) and licences (native animals only) for animals also varies. In some states, you need to be 16 years or older to get a licence. If you are not yet old enough, you will need the support of an adult to apply for the licence in their name.

In most states dogs and cats must be registered with the local council. Likewise, many states require that you have a licence to own native animals such as reptiles, amphibians, mammals and some birds. You don't need a licence for non-native pets such as rats, mice, guinea pigs and rabbits, although it is against the law to keep rabbits as pets in Queensland.

When you source a pet from an ethical place with high standards they will be able to explain the registration and licensing rules that apply to your animal. This information is also easy to access and check online.

**IF YOU ARE NOT YET OLD ENOUGH, YOU WILL NEED THE SUPPORT OF AN ADULT TO APPLY FOR THE LICENCE.**

28

# PETS AND ALLERGIES

So, you're an animal lover who can't resist cuddling cute creatures, right? But every time you get up-close to a furry friend, your eyes start to water, the annoying sneezing begins and you break out in itchy rashes.

Allergies to pet hair, fur, feathers, saliva and dander (tiny flecks of shed skin) are common. For some people the reaction is only mild, but for others it can be very serious. Interactive (hands-on) pets like dogs and cats cause the most problems. If you, or someone in your family suffers from allergies, a breed that sheds less (or has no hair at all) may be more suitable.

Many people who are allergic to dogs and cats are completely fine with other small animals such as rabbits, guinea pigs, rats, mice, budgies and cockatiels. If not, observational (hands-off) pets such as reptiles, fish and insects can sometimes make better pets for allergy sufferers. They do not shed hair and can be housed inside glass enclosures or aquariums.

Your pet depends on you keeping fit and healthy to care for them. If you have allergic reactions to animals always talk to a doctor about which pet is safest for you.

**MANY PEOPLE WHO ARE ALLERGIC TO DOGS AND CATS ARE COMPLETELY FINE WITH OTHER SMALL ANIMALS SUCH AS RABBITS, GUINEA PIGS, RATS, MICE, BUDGIES AND COCKATIELS.**

# HEALTH AND HYGIENE

Animals can carry germs and diseases. Some diseases are zoonotic (can transfer from animals to humans). There is no need to panic or worry about getting sick if you have good pet hygiene (cleanliness) habits and keep your animal healthy.

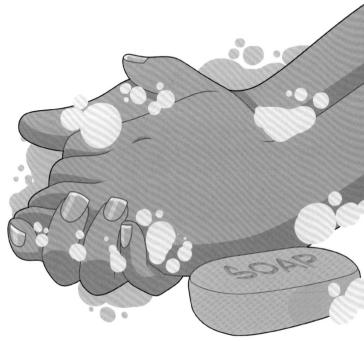

The golden rule of animal hygiene is: ALWAYS wash your hands before and after handling any pet. Use warm soapy water or hand-sanitising gel that you can keep beside your pet's enclosure.

Discourage your pet from walking on surfaces where you prepare or eat food. Wipe benches and tabletops with a pet safe disinfectant if they do. Tempting as it may seem, it is safer not to let an animal lick your face or eat food from your plate. Use a separate 'pet towel' for dirty paws and keep the floors you share clean.

Your pet's vaccinations and any parasite (tick, flea, worm) treatments should also be

**ALWAYS WASH YOUR HANDS BEFORE AND AFTER HANDLING ANY PET.**

• • • • • • • • • • • • •

kept up to date. Preferably wear gloves and use pet-safe detergent and disinfectant to regularly clean enclosures, bedding and pet accessories (food bowls, toys, leads, litter boxes etc.). Do this in an outside sink or bucket away from human family members.

30

# DEALING WITH THE PASSING OF A PET

Many animals have shorter lives than us. The hardest part about caring for a pet is dealing with the passing of our precious friends. Losing a pet is traumatic. It is sometimes our first experience with the death of someone we love deeply. Although I have experienced the loss of many treasured pets over the years, I still find it a very difficult time.

People react differently to the death of a pet. You may go through many emotions; sadness, loneliness, fear, frustration, anger, or even guilt. This is normal. Don't be embarrassed about the way you are feeling. There is no 'right' way to feel or act. It can help to talk to the adults in your life.

What gives me comfort when I'm trying to cope is to honour the life of my pet. I like to bury my animals at home and share favourite memories with my family. Other people prefer to write stories, draw pictures or frame a photo of their pet to keep close. These are all special ways to remember a

pet and you need to deal with your pet's loss in a way that feels right for you.

While the death of a pet is painful, try not to let it overwhelm you. Our pets are teaching us another important lesson: that death is a normal part of life. With time, you will work through your feelings and it will be the happy memories of your pet that last forever.

# PET PROPOSAL

After you've read the Pet Profiles, selected the pet you can best care for and prepared a Pet Budget you are ready to complete an impressive Pet Proposal to present to the adults in your life.

You will find a blank Pet Proposal form to copy at the back of this book. Here is one I have filled out as an example to show you how easy it is to do.

32

## PET PROPOSAL

**PREFERRED PET**
Pygmy Bearded Dragon

**LIFESPAN**
10–15 years

**SPACE NEEDED**
How much room does your pet need?
Where will your pet be housed at your home?
- 90 x 45 x 60 cm reptile enclosure.
- I will keep the enclosure in my bedroom.

**DIET**
What does your pet eat?
Where will you buy your pet's food from?
- Live insects, fruits and vegetables.
- We can buy the insects from the local pet store. We can buy the fruits and vegetables from the supermarket.

## CARE REQUIRED

When will you look after your pet? (before/after school)
How long will it take each day/week?

- I will clean my beardie's enclosure every morning before school. This will take around 5 minutes.
- I will give him fresh water and food each morning and again in the afternoon while he's a baby.
- I will fully replace the sand in his enclosure every 3–4 months.

## COST OF CARE

Attach your completed Pet Budget.

- My bearded dragon pet budget is attached.

## CONCERNS

Address any concerns the adults in your life may have about you getting this pet. Use the tips in the 'Convincing the adults' section in this book.

- 'Who will care for it when we go away?' My best friend has asked his parents and they are happy to look after the beardie when we go away.
- 'Beardies are expensive.' I have saved $300 pocket money. I'd also like to get money for my birthday to put towards getting a beardie.

# PET PLEDGE

Congratulations! You have worked hard reading, planning and gaining adult support to start an exciting new chapter in your life with a pet. Remember, don't let yourself, your adults, or most importantly your animal down by not delivering on being your pet's best friend.

Show your commitment by taking the Pet Pledge to be a responsible pet carer. By taking the Pet Pledge you promise not only to be the best 'pet parent' you can be, but you also agree to become an animal ambassador for all creatures and the environment.

Fill out the Pet Pledge at the back of your handbook, add a photo of you and your pet, hang it on your wall and live by these words. The time and love you invest in caring for animals and the environment will bring you the greatest happiness in life.

Let the fun begin ...

# PET PROFILES
## AN OVERVIEW

### FURRY PETS – MAMMALS

- Dogs
- Cats
- Mice and rats
- Guinea pigs
- Rabbits
- Spinifex hopping mice

### CREEPY CRAWLY PETS – CRITTERS

- Stick insects
- Giant burrowing cockroaches
- Scorpions
- Hermit crabs
- Silkworms
- Worm farm

36

## SCALY PETS – REPTILES

- Bearded dragons
- Pythons
- Blue-tongue lizards
- Turtles
- Geckos

## FEATHERED PETS – BIRDS

- Budgies
- Cockatiels
- Chickens
- Finches
- Quail

## WET PETS – FISH AND AMPHIBIANS

- Siamese fighting fish
- Goldfish
- Tropical fish
- Axolotls
- Frogs

# FURRY PETS — MAMMALS

## DOGS

**BREEDS:** Some of the best dog breeds for families include Cavalier King Charles spaniels, golden retrievers, labradors, beagles, cavoodles and labradoodles

**LIFESPAN:** 10–15 years

**SIZE:** There are toy, small, medium and large breeds

**MAINTENANCE LEVEL:** High

**COST:** $$$

38

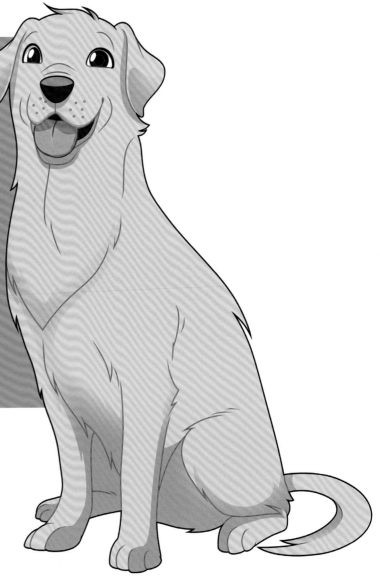

We love our dogs! In fact, dogs are the most popular pet in Australia. Dogs make wonderful pets and will give you their unconditional love. They are intelligent, loyal and affectionate animals. Deciding to bring a dog into your family is a huge decision and one that you will need to discuss with the whole family.

Ask yourself, does my family have the time, space and resources to devote to loving and giving a dog its best life? Am I prepared to put the needs of a dog before my own and spend time walking, playing and picking up poo every day?

If a dog is the right pet for you, consider whether adopting or fostering might be a suitable option. You will also need to think about whether you can properly care for: a large dog or a smaller dog, an energetic dog or a more relaxed dog, a dog that needs lots of grooming or a dog that doesn't shed much hair.

## HOUSING

Dogs love to be near you. Let your dog share your home and be part of the family action. When they can't be inside, make sure they have a secure area (fenced backyard, courtyard, verandah) to stretch out and snooze in. While some dogs live happily in apartments, many high-energy breeds need more room to run.

Your dog's living space should have plenty of shade and shelter including a kennel and bed to sleep in. Dog crates can also be useful to train, transport, or just give your special friend a quiet, safe place to take time out.

**AM I PREPARED TO PUT THE NEEDS OF A DOG BEFORE MY OWN AND SPEND TIME WALKING, PLAYING AND PICKING UP POO EVERY DAY?**

**DOGS ARE SUPER SMART SO YOUR BEST FRIEND NEEDS PLENTY OF INTERESTING TOYS TO KEEP THEM BUSY AND ENTERTAINED.**

· · · · · · · · · · · · · · ·

## EQUIPMENT

Your dog needs a collar, lead and dog tag engraved with their name and your contact details in case they get lost. You will also need sturdy food and water bowls and a travel harness or crate to keep your dog safe in the car.

Dogs are super smart so your best friend needs plenty of interesting toys (chew toys, soft toys, toys with hidden treats) to keep them busy and entertained, especially when you're not at home. Don't forget to change your dog's toys, or they'll get bored.

## MAINTENANCE

Wash, rinse and refresh your dog's water bowl every day and pick up any poo. You will also need to wash and groom your precious pooch to keep them looking and feeling their best. Use dog shampoo, conditioner, brushes and nail clippers to help you. Your puppy should be washed every 1–2 weeks with a special soap-free puppy shampoo. When your dog is older they should only be washed every 3–4 weeks. If you wash your dog too often, it can irritate their skin by removing natural oils. Dogs with longer coats, or that shed more often, will need to be brushed regularly.

Dogs require ongoing vaccinations to stay healthy. Puppies receive a series of vaccinations from 6 to 16 weeks and then all dogs should be taken to the vet for annual booster shots once a year. You will also need to treat your dog for fleas, ticks and worms. Talk to your vet, or local pet

### TALK TO YOUR VET, OR LOCAL PET STORE, ABOUT THE BEST PRODUCTS TO USE TO PROTECT YOUR DOG.

• • • • • • • • • • • • • •

store, about the best products to use to protect your dog. There are many health and behavioural benefits to having your dog desexed. A vet can provide you with more advice about this service.

Dogs thrive with training, regular exercise and lots of play time. I recommend you enrol your dog in puppy preschool. This is a great place to start socialising your dog with other pups and people. You will learn lots of new skills to make life together more enjoyable for you both.

As your dog grows, a daily walk, or two, is a must. Dog-friendly parks can be fun places to meet other dog-lovers and let your doggos burn off some energy. Don't forget to take biodegradable poo bags to clean up after your dog when you are out and about. I love getting home each day to spend time throwing a ball, giving tummy rubs and walking in the bush with my gorgeous labrador, Belle.

## DIET

Dogs are carnivores. Feed your dog on a premium dry or wet dog food for a complete, formulated diet with everything your dog needs to stay healthy. Offer raw meat and canned food from time to time for variety.

Use dog treats (packaged dry treats, uncooked bones) as a reward when training your dog, or to help clean their teeth. While you can never give your dog too much love, you can overfeed them. Remember not to let your dog get overweight, because this can lead to many health problems.

### BEN'S TOP TIP

Keep your dog cool in hot weather by adding ice cubes to their water bowl. For summertime fun try making a doggy 'ice block' by freezing your pup's favourite treats in a recycled plastic container filled with water. Many dogs also love a refreshing dip in a shallow wading pool on a hot day.

42

# CHECKLIST

- KENNEL, BED AND DOG CRATE
- COLLAR, LEAD AND PET TAG
- FOOD AND WATER BOWLS
- TRAVEL HARNESS
- FOOD
- TOYS
- BRUSH
- NAIL CLIPPERS
- SHAMPOO AND CONDITIONER
- FLEA, TICK AND WORMING TREATMENTS
- ANNUAL VACCINATIONS
- BIODEGRADABLE POO BAGS

## FUN FACT

Cuddling your dog is good for your health. When you give your dog a hug, a hormone called oxytocin is released in both your bodies. This hormone lowers your heart rate and blood pressure. So, don't forget to have your daily pooch snuggle to help you both live happier lives.

# CATS

**BREEDS:** Burmese, domestic shorthair, ragdoll and the Australian mist are all great cat breeds for children and families

**LIFESPAN:** 12–18 years

**SIZE:** 3–9 kg

**MAINTENANCE LEVEL:** Medium

**COST:** $$$

After dogs, cats are the second most popular pets in Australia. Cats are curious, independent, intelligent animals who make fun, interactive companions inside the home. While they may not need a daily walk like a dog, bringing a cat into your family is still a big commitment.

**SADLY, CATS ARE RESPONSIBLE FOR THE DEATHS OF BILLIONS (YES, THAT'S RIGHT ... BILLIONS!) OF NATIVE ANIMALS IN AUSTRALIA EVERY YEAR.**

## HOUSING

There are many reasons why your cat should live indoors. For one, you can keep them safe inside your home. Don't let your kitty-cat roam the streets or they might get hit by a car, catch a disease, or be injured in a cat fight with a less friendly feline.

Your cat should also be kept inside because they are natural born hunters. Sadly, cats are responsible for the deaths of billions (yes, that's right ... billions!) of native animals in Australia every year. Most people are unaware that the average pet cat kills around 75 native animals each year. While cats make amazing pets, we must protect our native wildlife and educate others to do the same by keeping cats indoors.

If you would like to let your cat enjoy spending time outside there are many secure outdoor 'catteries' and enclosures available. Why not connect the cattery to your house so your cat can move between the inside and outside of your home as they please.

## EQUIPMENT

Your cat needs a collar and pet tag engraved with their name and your contact details in case they get lost. A food and water bowl and a litter tray with environmentally friendly kitty litter for toileting are also basic cat essentials. Provide your cat with a bed and access to

45

**IF YOU WOULD LIKE TO LET YOUR CAT ENJOY SPENDING TIME OUTSIDE THERE ARE MANY SECURE OUTDOOR 'CATTERIES' AND ENCLOSURES AVAILABLE.**

• • • • • • • • • • • • • • •

an enclosed, dark place to retreat to and feel secure, or to sleep. It's also important to have a pet carrier to safely transport your cat in the car.

Cats are very playful, so you'll need lots of toys to keep them entertained, especially when you're not at home. Don't forget to change their toys, or they'll get bored. Encourage your cat to use a scratching post instead of the furniture.

## MAINTENANCE

Wash, rinse and refresh your cat's water bowl every day. Remove any poo from the litter tray and completely replace the kitty litter 1–2 times each week or it will start to smell. Cats are very clean animals and spend large amounts of time each day grooming themselves. You will still need to brush your cat using a special brush designed for cat fur. Long-haired breeds need more grooming than short-haired breeds.

Treat your cat for fleas, ticks and worms. Speak to your vet or local pet store about which treatments are best and how to give them to your cat.

## DIET

Cats are carnivores. Feed your cat on a mix of premium dry cat food and wet canned food. Regularly offer raw meat and raw, fleshy bones as part of a varied diet. Your adult cat will usually prefer to graze and eat smaller meals throughout the day. You should also have some treats (dried meat, fish and dental chews) to use as rewards and to help keep your cat's teeth clean. Cats also enjoy plants (pet grass, or catnip) to eat, but ensure any indoor plants are not toxic for your kitty.

46

## BEN'S TOP TIP

Get creative and make some simple, fun toys for your cat. A large cardboard box with holes cut in it can provide hours of entertainment. You could also dangle some cut-out felt shapes on a stick to encourage natural pouncing behaviour.

## FUN FACT

Cats sleep up to 15 hours each day. Cats are crepuscular animals, which means they are most active in the early morning and evenings. By sleeping for long periods they conserve energy. So, why not snuggle up and have a 'cat nap' with your feline friend.

48

# CHECKLIST

- OUTDOOR CATTERY
- COLLAR AND PET TAG
- FOOD AND WATER BOWL
- LITTER TRAY AND KITTY LITTER
- PET CARRIER
- BED
- TOYS
- SCRATCHING POST
- CAT BRUSH
- FOOD AND TREATS
- FLEA, TICK AND WORMING TREATMENTS

# MICE AND RATS

**LIFESPAN:** 2–3 years

**SIZE:** Mice: 7–10 cm (body length);
rats: 22–25 cm (body length)

**MAINTENANCE LEVEL:** Low

**COST:** $

Mice and rats, also known as rodents, are cute, compact pets who don't take up a lot of room. Although small, mice and rats are super smart, energetic and affectionate. Gently handling your mice and rats every day will help you develop a special bond with your animals, but you will need to have quick hands because they can move fast.

**A DARK HIDE WILL PROVIDE THE PERFECT PLACE FOR YOUR MICE AND RATS TO SLEEP AND MAKE THEIR NEST.**

Mice and rats are very active and love to climb and explore. Look for an enclosure with multiple levels and tunnels to keep your little friends busy. Position the enclosure away from draughts and direct sunlight, as mice and rats are very sensitive to extreme cold or heat. Your rodents will be happy and stay healthy if you keep them at temperatures between 18 and 26 °C.

## HOUSING

Your mice and rats are best housed in a purpose-built wire rodent enclosure. Rodents are very social creatures, so should be kept in pairs. If you don't want your mice and rats to breed, keep two of the same sex together (ideally females as males may fight). For two mice, you will need an enclosure at least 45 x 30 x 30 cm and for two rats, 70 x 40 x 45 cm (or larger).

## EQUIPMENT

You will need a ceramic food bowl and a water bottle with a dripper to attach to the inside of the enclosure. Spread recycled paper pellets across the floor of their enclosure as absorbent bedding. Never use wood shavings as they contain dust that can make your rodent sick. A dark hide will provide the perfect place for your mice and rats to sleep and make their nest.

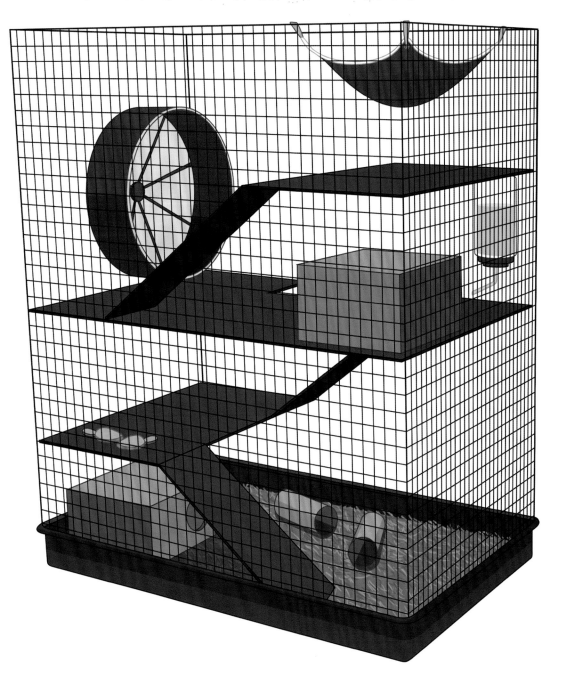

You should also give your rodents dried grass or shredded newspaper to use as a nesting material.

Mice and rats are inquisitive creatures who love to chew. In fact, they need to chew to grind down their constantly growing incisors (front teeth). Offer them plenty of toys (safe wood chew toys, toilet rolls, ladders, tunnels and a running wheel) for hours of exercise and entertainment.

## MAINTENANCE

Wash, rinse and refresh your rodent's water bowl every day. Completely replace their bedding 1–2 times each week. Wipe over their enclosure, toys and sleeping areas with a rodent-safe disinfectant. If you don't keep their

## MICE AND RATS ARE INQUISITIVE CREATURES WHO LOVE TO CHEW

• • • • • • • • • • • • • • • • • •

enclosure clean it will smell and your animals could get sick. You will also need to worm your mice and rats by adding a small-animal worming solution to their water every three months.

## DIET

Make sure your rodents always have plenty of high-quality mouse or rat pellets to eat. They also need fresh vegetables and fruit (corn, beans, peas, broccoli, endive, carrot and apple) every day. You can offer them treats (seeds, nuts and even mealworms) 1–2 times a week.

53

## BEN'S TOP TIP

Never keep mice and rats together in the same enclosure. Although they may look alike, they will definitely fight, and prefer the company of their own species.

## FUN FACT

Mice and rats are highly intelligent.
Rats can solve problems and learn new tricks as quickly as a dog.

# CHECKLIST

- WIRE RODENT ENCLOSURE
- CERAMIC FOOD BOWL
- WATER BOTTLE WITH A DRIPPER
- HIDE
- BEDDING
- NESTING MATERIAL
- TOYS AND CHEWS
- FOOD
- WORMING SOLUTION
- DISINFECTANT

# GUINEA PIGS

**BREEDS:** Short-haired, crested and sheltie

......................................................

**LIFESPAN:** 5–8 years

......................................................

**SIZE:** 20–25 cm

......................................................

**MAINTENANCE LEVEL:** Medium

......................................................

**COST:** $$

Guinea pigs are packed with personality. They are calm, confident, friendly animals, who are usually easy to handle. They are also very social and should be kept in pairs. Guinea pigs enjoy gentle cuddles and plenty of time outside their enclosure. If you're looking for some little furry friends to brush and play with every day, gorgeous guinea pigs might be the perfect pets for you.

**IF YOU'RE LOOKING FOR SOME LITTLE FURRY FRIENDS TO BRUSH AND PLAY WITH EVERY DAY, GORGEOUS GUINEA PIGS MIGHT BE THE PERFECT PETS FOR YOU.**

Ensure outdoor hutches are secure to protect your guinea pigs from predators like cats and dogs.

Guinea pigs don't cope well in temperatures over 25 degrees. They are happiest when kept in temperatures between 18 and 22 °C, so make sure their outdoor hutch gets plenty of shade in summer. Having outdoor and indoor housing options will allow you to move your guinea pigs to the most suitable environment, depending on the weather.

## HOUSING

You can comfortably house guinea pigs in a large outdoor guinea pig or rabbit hutch, an indoor enclosure, or both. Hutches and enclosures come in many different shapes, sizes and materials. If you don't want your guinea pigs to breed, make sure you house two females together. Their hutch or enclosure should be at least 120 x 60 x 60 cm, although bigger is better.

## EQUIPMENT

You will need a ceramic food bowl and a water bottle with a dripper to attach to the inside of the hutch. Spread soft and absorbent bedding (wood shavings) on the floor of their hutch. Provide a dark hide and a sheltered area for your guinea pigs to sleep and feel safe.

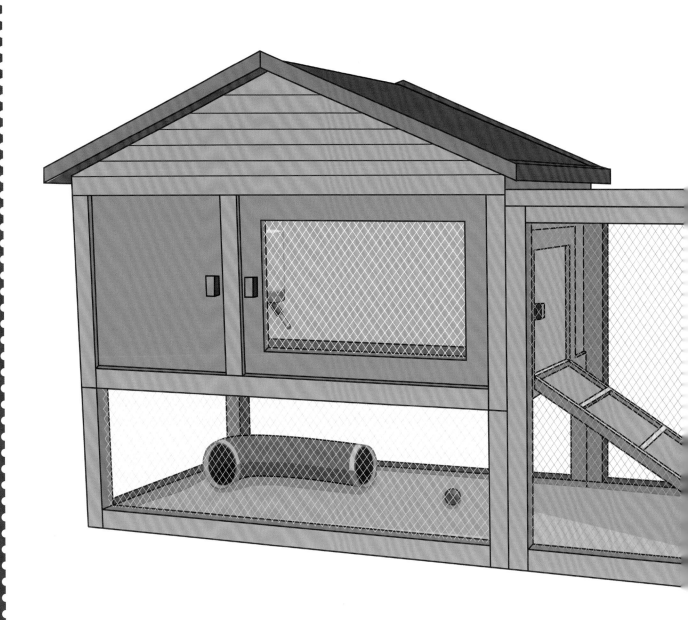

**GUINEA PIGS ENJOY INTERACTING WITH YOU AND THEIR ENVIRONMENT.**

You can also spread straw inside their sleeping area for comfort.

Offer your guinea pigs plenty of toys (wooden chew toys, woven toys and even plastic cat balls with bells inside) to keep them busy and entertained.

## MAINTENANCE

Wash, rinse and refresh your guinea pig's water bowl every day. Remove any poo or uneaten food to keep their hutch clean and dry. Completely replace their bedding at least once a week. Wipe over their enclosure, toys and sleeping areas with a small-animal-safe disinfectant. Don't forget to worm your guinea pigs by giving them a small-animal worming solution every three months.

Guinea pigs enjoy interacting with you and their environment. Take them out of their enclosure for at least an hour each day. Give them time on the floor, inside a pen, or take them outside on the grass if it's not too hot.

59

Never leave your guinea pigs alone or they might wander away or chew on something they shouldn't. Groom your guinea pigs by gently brushing them at least twice a week.

## DIET

Make sure your guinea pigs always have plenty of grass hay (Western Timothy hay, oaten hay, or lucerne for guinea pigs under 6 months) to eat. You should also give them a bowl of specially formulated guinea pig pellets and fresh vegetables and fruits that are high in vitamin C (capsicum, kale, carrot, broccoli, corn and apple) every day. Hang a salt and mineral stone from the side of the hutch for the guinea pigs to lick.

## FUN FACT

Guinea pigs are also known as 'cavies' and originally came from South America. They were domesticated over 3000 years ago, originally as a source of food, and were only later kept as pets.

## BEN'S TOP TIP

Unlike humans, guinea pigs are unable to make their own vitamin C. It's very important to give them lots of vegetables and fruits that are high in vitamin C and a pelleted diet containing vitamin C. Without enough of this important vitamin they will get sick.

# CHECKLIST

- CERAMIC FOOD BOWL
- WATER BOTTLE WITH A DRIPPER
- HIDE
- BEDDING
- TOYS AND CHEWS
- FOOD
- SALT AND MINERAL STONE
- WORMING SOLUTION
- DISINFECTANT

# RABBITS

**BREEDS:** Popular breeds include dwarf lop and miniature lop

**LIFESPAN:** 5–10 years

**SIZE:** Dwarf lop: 1.9–2.4 kg; miniature lop: 1.5 kg

**MAINTENANCE LEVEL:** Medium

**COST:** $$

—FURRY PETS

Rabbits are adorable and fun pets that love to play. They are very clean and easy to litter train. They are also very social and should be kept in pairs. However, rabbits don't always tolerate being handled well. They can be nervous and scratchy if they don't want to be held. I would only recommend rabbits as pets if you are a bit older and have plenty of time to devote to your bouncy friend.

**NOTE: IT IS AGAINST THE LAW TO KEEP RABBITS AS PETS IF YOU LIVE IN QUEENSLAND.**

· · · · · · · · · · · · ·

## HOUSING

You can comfortably house rabbits in a large rabbit hutch. Hutches come in many different shapes, sizes and materials. For two rabbits your hutch should be no smaller than 180 x 70 x 60 cm. Some hutches have large exercise areas attached to them. The bigger the enclosure, the better it is for your rabbits. You can keep a male and female together, but they must both be desexed, otherwise you will end up with more bunnies than you bargained for.

Rabbits are happiest when kept at temperatures between 18 and 22 °C. Ideally, it is good to have indoor and outdoor housing options. This will allow you to bring your rabbits inside when it is too hot, or too cold. Make sure your outdoor hutch closes securely to protect your rabbits from predators like cats and dogs, and gets plenty of shade in summer.

## EQUIPMENT

You will need a ceramic food bowl and a water bottle with a dripper to attach to the inside of the hutch. Spread soft and absorbent bedding (wood shavings) on the floor. Provide a dark hide and a sheltered area for your rabbits to feel safe and have somewhere to sleep. Use straw inside their sleeping area to make them comfortable.

Use a litter tray to toilet-train your rabbit and keep their droppings in one place.

Rabbits need to chew to help keep their teeth filed down and healthy. Offer them plenty of toys (wooden chew toys, woven toys). Tunnels and ramps are also great for keeping them busy and entertained.

## MAINTENANCE

Wash, rinse and refresh your rabbit's water bowl every day. Remove any poo or uneaten food to keep their hutch clean and dry. Completely replace their bedding at least once a week. Wipe over their enclosure, toys and sleeping areas with a small-animal-safe disinfectant. Don't forget to worm your rabbits using a small-animal worming solution every three months. You will also need to take them to the vet to be vaccinated against calicivirus once a year.

Rabbits need lots of time outside their enclosure to exercise and explore every day.

## NEVER LEAVE YOUR RABBITS ALONE OR THEY MIGHT WANDER AWAY OR CHEW SOMETHING THEY SHOULDN'T.

• • • • • • • • • • •

Let them out on the floor, put them inside a pen, or take them outside on the grass if it's not too hot. Never leave your rabbits alone or they might wander away or chew something they shouldn't. Groom your rabbits by gently brushing them every day.

## DIET

Make sure your rabbits always have plenty of grass hay (Western Timothy hay or oaten hay). You should also give them a bowl of specially formulated rabbit pellets and fresh vegetables and fruits (capsicum, kale, carrot, broccoli, corn and apple) every day. Hang a salt and mineral stone from the side of their hutch for your rabbits to lick.

## FUN FACT

Rabbits eat their own poo.
By re-digesting their food,
rabbits get a second chance
to absorb any nutrients they
might have missed the first time
around. Gross!

## BEN'S TOP TIP

A rabbit's teeth continue to
grow for their entire life. Make
sure you give your rabbit
plenty of wooden chew toys
so that they can file their teeth
down naturally.

## CHECKLIST

- HUTCH
- CERAMIC FOOD BOWL
- WATER BOTTLE WITH A DRIPPER
- LITTER TRAY
- HIDE
- BEDDING
- TOYS, CHEWS, TUNNELS AND RAMPS
- FOOD
- SALT AND MINERAL STONE
- WORMING SOLUTION
- DISINFECTANT

# SPINIFEX HOPPING MICE

**LIFESPAN:** 3–4 years

**SIZE:** Up to 14 cm (Including tail)

**MAINTENANCE LEVEL:** Medium

**COST:** $$

Spinifex hopping mice are a native species of rodent found throughout central Australia. They make unique pets. They are very busy and bouncy (as their name suggests) so you can't handle them like domestic mice, but they're fascinating creatures to watch.

NOTE: YOU WILL NEED A MAMMAL KEEPER'S LICENCE TO CARE FOR HOPPING MICE AS PETS IN NEW SOUTH WALES AND VICTORIA. A LICENCE IS NOT REQUIRED TO KEEP THEM IN SOUTH AUSTRALIA AND THE NORTHERN TERRITORY. UNFORTUNATELY, YOU CAN'T KEEP HOPPING MICE IF YOU LIVE IN QUEENSLAND, TASMANIA OR WESTERN AUSTRALIA.

• • • • • • • • • • • • • •

## HOUSING

You can house spinifex hopping mice in a glass enclosure (a reptile enclosure is ideal) which is secure, well ventilated and easy to access for cleaning and maintenance. Keep a small group of 2 or 3 hopping mice in a 90 x 45 x 60 cm enclosure, or up to 6 adult mice in a larger 120 x 45 x 60 cm enclosure.

Position their enclosure away from draughts and direct sunlight. Your hopping mice are very sensitive and can't cope with extreme cold or heat. They are happiest when housed at temperatures between 18 and 26 °C.

## EQUIPMENT

You will need a ceramic food bowl and a water bottle with a dripper to attach to the inside of the enclosure. Hopping mice love to dig and burrow so spread a deep substrate (bedding) of desert sand across the floor of the enclosure. Provide a nesting box and nesting material (dry grass or straw) for your hopping mice to nest with, to feel safe, and to sleep in during the day.

Check the temperature of their enclosure with a thermometer. If the temperature drops below 18 °C you will need to put a heat lamp or heat mat at one end of the enclosure to keep your mice warm in winter.

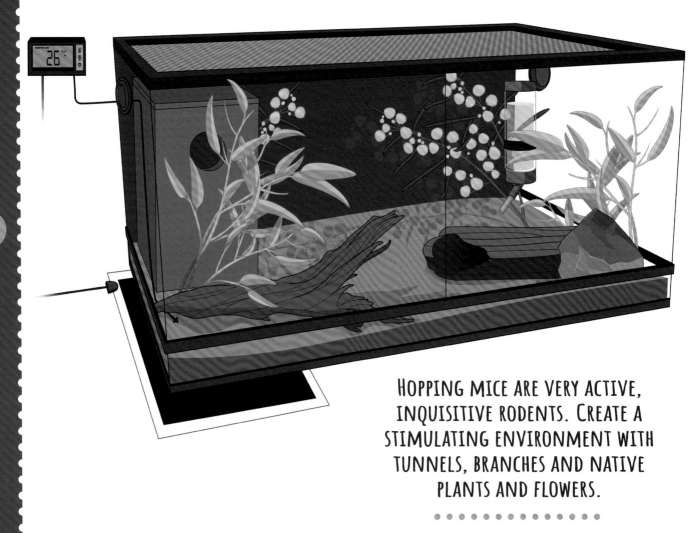

26 ℃

HOPPING MICE ARE VERY ACTIVE,
INQUISITIVE RODENTS. CREATE A
STIMULATING ENVIRONMENT WITH
TUNNELS, BRANCHES AND NATIVE
PLANTS AND FLOWERS.

## MAINTENANCE

Wash, rinse and refresh your rodent's water bottle every day. Remove any poo or uneaten food. Completely replace the substrate every 2–3 weeks. Wipe over their enclosure, nesting box and sleeping areas with a small-animal-safe disinfectant.

Hopping mice are very active, inquisitive rodents. Create a stimulating environment with tunnels, branches and native plants and flowers (eucalyptus, grevillea and bottlebrush) to keep your mice busy and entertained. Add pieces of timber and hollow logs because your hopping mice love to chew.

Hopping mice can be very jumpy and don't enjoy being handled too often. When you need to catch them to clean their enclosure, gently guide them into a small, well-ventilated, plastic tub where they can safely stay for a short period.

Don't forget to worm your hopping mice by adding a small-animal worming solution to their water every three months.

## DIET

Spinifex hopping mice are omnivores. Make sure they always have plenty of high-quality mouse or rat pellets. Mix small amounts of seed and grains with their pellets, such as cockatiel mix. Offer a range of fresh vegetables and fruits (sweet potato, peas, carrot and apple) every day.

Your mice will also need live insects (crickets, mealworms and black soldier fly larvae) 2–3 times a week. Hang a salt and mineral stone in their enclosure for them to lick.

## BEN'S TOP TIP

Like domestic mice, native hopping mice are great breeders. If you don't want to be overrun by these bouncing bundles of fur, make sure you only keep females together.

## FUN FACT

Spinifex hopping mice have enormous ears.
Living in a harsh desert environment, large ears are not only useful for helping the mice to hear predators approaching, but also for keeping cool.

## CHECKLIST

- GLASS ENCLOSURE
- CERAMIC FOOD BOWL
- WATER BOTTLE WITH A DRIPPER
- SUBSTRATE
- NESTING BOX
- TUNNELS, BRANCHES, NATIVE FLOWERS AND LOGS
- FOOD
- SALT AND MINERAL STONE
- WORMING SOLUTION
- DISINFECTANT

# SCALY PETS — REPTILES

## BEARDED DRAGON

**SPECIES:** Central and pygmy bearded dragon

**LIFESPAN:** 10–15 years

**SIZE:** 25–30 cm (pygmy), 50–60 cm (central)

**MAINTENANCE LEVEL:** Medium

**COST:** $$$

74

Bearded dragons (beardies) are sun-loving Australian desert reptiles who enjoy spending plenty of time basking each day. They are very friendly lizards who will happily come out of their enclosure and interact with you. Beardies come in many beautiful colours and are long lived.

## HOUSING

Beardies are solitary animals that should be housed on their own or they will probably fight (and that never ends well). I recommend a glass or timber reptile enclosure measuring at least 90 x 45 x 60 cm for one adult pygmy bearded dragon and 120 x 45 x 60 cm for one adult central bearded dragon. Their enclosure needs to allow plenty of airflow (fish tanks are not suitable) and have a secure door.

Inside the enclosure there should be a log or rock for your beardie to bask on, artificial plants and water and food bowls. Absorbent substrate (bedding) such as reptile-safe desert sand or an artificial grass mat is also important.

## BEARDED DRAGONS ARE ECTOTHERMS, WHICH MEANS THEY HEAT THEMSELVES UP USING THE SUN.

## EQUIPMENT

Bearded dragons are ectotherms, which means they heat themselves up using the sun. In captivity, your beardie will need a day basking globe (inside a light fitting) to keep warm. A thermostat should be used to control the temperature of the enclosure by turning the globe on and off as needed.

Set up your beardie enclosure to have a warm end and a cooler end. The warm end should be kept at temperatures around 40 °C. A basking log will allow your beardie to move closer to the heat if it is cold. The temperature at the cooler end should be kept between 24 and 26 °C and never drop below 18 and 21 °C at night. It is very important for you to check the temperatures every day. If your beardie gets too cold, or too hot, it will become sick.

Bearded dragons also need ultraviolet light (UV light) to grow and stay healthy. In the wild they get UV light from the sun. A reptile UVB globe or tube (inside a light fitting) will need to be placed on top of your beardie enclosure and run for 12 hours each day.

**KEEP YOUR BEARDIE ENCLOSURE CLEAN BY REMOVING ANY POO, SHED SKIN OR UNEATEN FOOD EVERY DAY.**

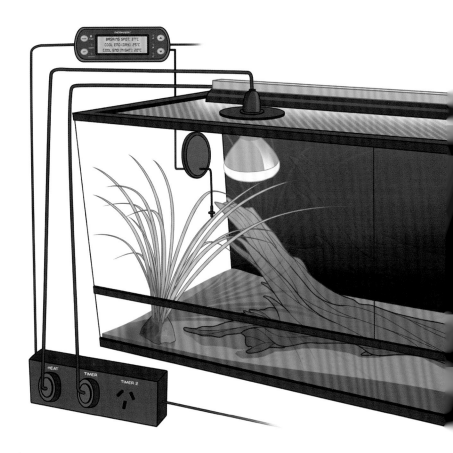

You should also take your beardie outside to enjoy natural sunlight a few times a week. Put your beardie in a mesh sunning enclosure to ensure it won't run off. Always stay with your beardie and don't leave them alone in full sun as they can overheat very quickly.

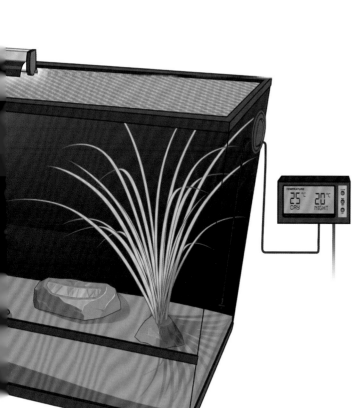

## MAINTENANCE

Keep your beardie enclosure clean by removing any poo, shed skin or uneaten food every day. Their water and food bowls should also be washed with a reptile disinfectant and refreshed daily. Completely replace their bedding every 3–4 months.

## DIET

Bearded dragons are omnivores and eat live insects (crickets, wood roaches, black soldier fly larvae, silkworms, and for adults as a treat, mealworms), vegetables (kale, endive, parsley, Asian greens, carrot, beans, zucchini and squash) and some fruits (apple, pear). Dust live foods with a calcium and vitamin powder before feeding them to your beardie. You can also sprinkle lizard pellets through the veggie mix.

While your bearded dragon is young and growing rapidly, feed it insects twice a day and veggies every morning. By the time your beardie is 12 months old they will have reached their adult size and you can offer them food every second day.

## FUN FACT

Bearded dragons have three eyes. The third eye, called the 'parietal eye', is a clear scale on the top of the beardie's head that acts as a sensor. This sensor takes in light and tells the dragon's body what time of day and year it is, stimulating them to breed in spring as the days become longer.

## BEN'S TOP TIP

You might feel uncomfortable about keeping one bearded dragon on its own. Don't stress! Bearded dragons prefer to live alone and don't need the company of other lizards. I discovered this the hard way. When I was young, I kept two bearded dragons together and one day I came home from school to find that the larger beardie had eaten its smaller sibling.

# CHECKLIST

- REPTILE ENCLOSURE
- DAY BASKING GLOBE
- UVB GLOBE OR TUBE
- THERMOSTAT
- BASKING LOG OR ROCK
- FOOD AND WATER BOWLS
- ARTIFICIAL PLANTS
- SUBSTRATE
- FOOD
- CALCIUM AND VITAMIN POWDER
- REPTILE DISINFECTANT
- MESH SUNNING ENCLOSURE

# PYTHON

**SPECIES: Children's python, spotted python and Stimson's python**

LIFESPAN: 20+ years

SIZE: 80–120 cm

MAINTENANCE
LEVEL: Low

COST: $$

Pythons are calm, gentle animals that are easy to handle and totally cool. Requiring much less frequent feeding, cleaning and enrichment than many other animals, pythons make a great alternative pet. With proper care, pythons are very long-lived. I still have my first pet snake, 'Rosie' the children's python, who is now 22 years old.

## HOUSING

You can house an adult children's python in a glass or timber reptile enclosure measuring 90 x 45 x 60 cm. However, your hatchling (baby) python will need to be kept in something much smaller (45 x 30 x 15 cm) for the first 12 months. Don't be tempted to keep your young snake in a big

enclosure because they will become stressed. Their enclosure needs to allow plenty of airflow (fish tanks are not suitable) and have a secure door.

Provide your python with branches for climbing and basking, a hide, artificial plants and a water bowl. Use an absorbent substrate (bedding) such as coconut fibre or aspen on the floor of the enclosure.

## EQUIPMENT

Pythons are ectotherms, which means they heat themselves up using the sun. In captivity, your python will need a ceramic heat emitter (and fitting) to keep warm. A thermostat should be used to control the temperature of the enclosure by turning the ceramic heat emitter on and off as needed.

Your python's enclosure needs a warm end and a cooler end. The warm end should be

**YOU SHOULD TAKE YOUR PYTHON OUTSIDE TO ENJOY NATURAL SUNLIGHT A FEW TIMES A WEEK.**

kept at temperatures between 28 and 32 °C. The climbing branch will allow your python to move closer to the heat if it is cold. Keep the temperature at the cooler end between 22 and 26 °C and never let it drop below 18–21 °C at night. It is very important for you to check the temperatures every day. If your python gets too cold, or too hot, it will become sick.

Pythons need access to ultraviolet light (UV light) to grow and stay healthy. In the wild they get UV light from the sun. A reptile UVB globe or tube will need to be placed on top of your python's enclosure and run for 12 hours each day. You should also take your python outside to enjoy natural sunlight a few times a week. Always stay with your snake to keep it safe and be very careful not to let your friend overheat.

## MAINTENANCE

Your python will usually do a poo about a week after you feed it. Keep their enclosure clean by removing this poo and any shed skin. Regularly wash their water bowl with a reptile disinfectant and completely replace the substrate every 2–3 months.

## DIET

Feed your python on thawed, frozen mice which you can purchase from a pet store. The size of the rodent you use will depend on the age and size of your snake. Hatchling pythons can be fed one small 'pinkie' mouse every week. As your snake grows you can progress to feeding them larger mice and an adult python can be fed every 2–3 weeks.

I feed my snakes in a separate plastic feeding tub. By doing this, my snakes don't think they're going to be fed every time I open their enclosure. I also suggest using feeding tongs to offer rodents to your python so your snake doesn't start associating your hand with food. It's better not to handle your python for a few days after it has been fed to allow it to digest its meal. It's also a good idea to keep a record of when your python eats and sheds its skin.

### HATCHLING PYTHONS CAN BE FED ONE SMALL 'PINKIE' MOUSE EVERY WEEK.

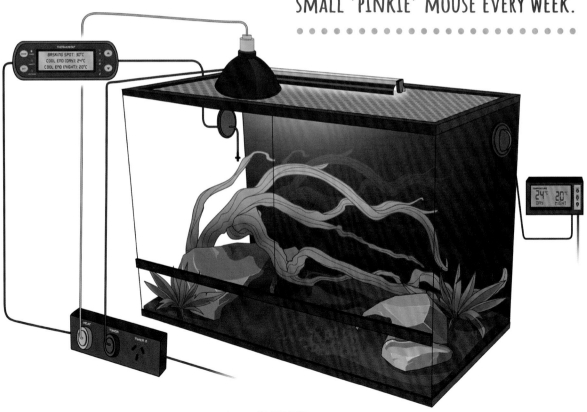

## FUN FACT

Why is a snake's tongue forked? Snakes use their tongue to pick up scent particles from the air. The fork provides them with more accurate information about the direction of food, or a mate.

## CHECKLIST

- REPTILE ENCLOSURE
- CERAMIC HEAT EMITTER
- UVB GLOBE OR TUBE
- THERMOSTAT
- CLIMBING BRANCH
- HIDE
- WATER BOWL
- SUBSTRATE
- FOOD
- REPTILE DISINFECTANT
- FEEDING TUB
- FEEDING TONGS

## BEN'S TOP TIP

A young python will shed its skin every 4–6 weeks. Before they shed they may refuse food and you will notice their scales become dull and their eyes may go a greyish colour. During this time gently mist your snake with some water once a day to help it have a perfect shed every time.

# BLUE-TONGUE LIZARD

**SPECIES:** Eastern blue-tongue lizard

**LIFESPAN:** 20+ years

**SIZE:** 40–60 cm

**MAINTENANCE LEVEL:** Medium

**COST:** $$$

Blue-tongues are large, gentle Australian native skinks that you may find living in your backyard. Blueys are very calm, easy to handle and make a fascinating reptile pet. With proper care, you and your bluey will live a long, happy life together.

## HOUSING

Blue-tongues are solitary animals and should be housed on their own otherwise they often fight. I recommend a glass or timber reptile enclosure measuring 120 x 45 x 60 cm to house one adult blue-tongue lizard. Their enclosure needs to allow plenty of airflow (fish tanks are not suitable) and have secure doors.

Provide your bluey with a log or rock for basking, artificial plants and water and food bowls.

Use absorbent substrate (bedding) such as coconut fibre, or an artificial grass mat on the floor of their enclosure.

## EQUIPMENT

Blue-tongues are ectotherms, which means they heat themselves up using the sun. In captivity, your bluey will need a reptile basking globe (and fitting) to keep warm. A thermostat should be used to control the temperature of the enclosure by switching the globe on and off as needed.

Your bluey's enclosure needs a warm end and a cooler end. The warm end should be kept at temperatures between 30 and 33 °C. The basking log or rock will allow your blue-tongue to move closer to the heat if it is cold. Keep the cooler end between 24 and 26 °C and never let it drop below 18–21 °C at night. It is very important for you to check the temperatures using a thermometer every day. If your bluey gets too cold, or too hot, it will become sick.

Blue-tongues also need access to ultraviolet light (UV light) to grow and stay

**BLUEYS ARE VERY CALM, EASY TO HANDLE AND MAKE A FASCINATING REPTILE PET.**

healthy. In the wild they get UV light from the sun. A reptile UVB globe or tube will need to be placed on top of the enclosure and run for 12 hours each day. You should also take your blue-tongue outside to enjoy natural sunlight a few times a week. Putting your bluey in a mesh sunning enclosure will ensure it won't run off. Always stay with your bluey and make sure they have access to shade, as they can overheat very quickly.

## MAINTENANCE

Keep your blue-tongue's enclosure clean by doing a daily check and removing any poo, shed skin or uneaten food. Their water and food bowls should also be washed with a reptile disinfectant and refreshed daily. Completely replace your bluey's bedding every 2–3 months.

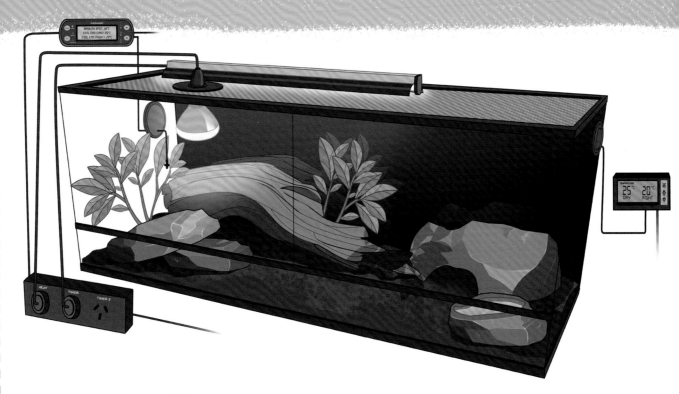

## WHILE YOUR BLUEY IS YOUNG AND GROWING RAPIDLY FEED IT EVERY DAY.

## DIET

Blue-tongues are omnivores and eat live insects (crickets, snails, black soldier fly larvae, silkworms and mealworms only as a treat) and fruits and vegetables (apple, pear, melons, pitted stone fruits, berries, banana, squash, carrot, endive and kale). You can also sprinkle lizard pellets through the fruit and veggie mix and offer tinned dog and cat food (beef or chicken), or a boiled egg as a tasty treat. Dust live and tinned foods with a calcium and vitamin powder before feeding them to your bluey.

While your bluey is young and growing rapidly feed it every day. By the time your lizard is 10–12 months old they will have reached their adult size and you can offer them food every two or three days.

# CHECKLIST

- REPTILE ENCLOSURE
- BASKING GLOBE
- UVB GLOBE OR TUBE
- THERMOSTAT AND THERMOMETER
- BASKING LOG
- FOOD AND WATER BOWLS
- SUBSTRATE
- FOOD
- CALCIUM AND VITAMIN POWDER
- REPTILE DISINFECTANT
- MESH SUNNING ENCLOSURE

## BEN'S TOP TIP

Blue-tongues love snails and snails are often out and about after rain. Why not try collecting some to feed to your lizard? Just check your parents and neighbours have not put any snail baits or pesticides down in their gardens. If your lizard eats a snail that has ingested a poisonous bait, it could become very sick.

## FUN FACT

Why do blue-tongue lizards have blue tongues?
If threatened by a predator, blue-tongues quickly open their mouth, flatten out their tongue and hiss loudly. The bright blue colour startles the predator, potentially saving the lizard's life.

# TURTLE

**SPECIES: Eastern long-necked turtle, Murray short-necked turtle and Macleay River turtle**

**LIFESPAN: 50–60 years**

**SIZE: 30–40 cm (shell size)**

**MAINTENANCE LEVEL: High**

**COST: $$$**

Turtles are totally terrific. They have their own unique personalities and can even learn to recognise you. But please think very carefully before bringing a turtle into your life because they are a time-consuming pet. If you are willing to put in the extra effort and you're looking for a forever friend, a turtle could be right for you. If you care for your turtle well, you could get to share the next 50 years with your mate.

## HOUSING

Turtles are solitary animals who should be housed on their own, otherwise they may fight or bully each other. You can house your turtle in a 120 x 60 x 60 cm aquarium or turtle tank for its lifetime, although Murray short-necked turtles require a larger 180 x 60 x 60 cm tank as they grow very big. A smaller 60 x 45 x 45 cm (minimum) tank can be used for a small hatchling turtle for the first year. Turtles grow very fast and get big so it's important that they have plenty of room to swim around.

Your turtle needs a dry dock (land area) to bask on. Their tank should also have coarse gravel or pebbles on the base of the tank, a secure mesh lid and some plants and driftwood for the turtle to hide amongst to feel safe.

> **TURTLES GROW VERY FAST AND GET BIG SO IT'S IMPORTANT THAT THEY HAVE PLENTY OF ROOM TO SWIM AROUND.**

Your turtle also needs ultraviolet light (UV light) to stay healthy and maintain a hard shell. In the wild they get UV light from the sun. A reptile UVB tube will need to be placed on top of their enclosure and run for 12 hours each day. You can also take your turtle outside to enjoy natural sunlight a few times a week. Be careful not to over-handle your turtle, particularly as a hatchling, as they can get stressed easily.

You will also need a strong filter to help keep your tank clean. Some turtle tanks come with their own built-in filtration systems, otherwise I would recommend you use a canister filter.

## EQUIPMENT

To keep your turtle healthy you need to provide two sources of heat. Use an aquarium water heater to maintain the water temperature between 22 and 26 °C. Check your tank water temperature daily using a thermometer. You will also need to position a splash-proof basking globe (and fitting) above your turtle's dry dock. The perfect basking temperature for a turtle is between 28 and 32 °C.

## MAINTENANCE

Turtles are very messy animals. You will need to remove and replace about 30% of their tank water with fresh water every week. Don't forget to add water conditioner to any new tap water to ensure it is safe for your turtle. The gravel will also need to be vacuumed using an aquarium siphon. I vacuum each week when I freshen up the tank water, to get rid of any turtle poop in the gravel.

## DIET

A varied diet will keep your little friend in tip-top-turtle condition. Remember, long-necked turtles are carnivores and short-necked turtles are omnivores. Feed your turtle live foods (crickets, bloodworms, earthworms, feeder fish and small yabbies), frozen turtle food and turtle pellets. Don't forget to coat live insects in calcium and vitamin powder. Short-necked turtles often enjoy feeding on live aquarium plants and some leafy greens (like kale).

Feed your hatchling turtle every day. When your turtle is 1 or 2 years old you can offer them food every 2 to 3 days. It's a good idea to feed your turtle in a separate feeding tub with a little of their tank water because they are such messy eaters.

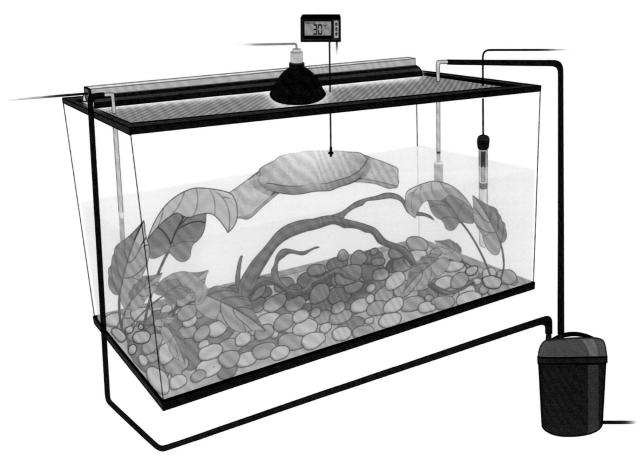

## CHECKLIST

- TURTLE TANK
- AQUARIUM WATER HEATER
- BASKING GLOBE
- UVB TUBE
- THERMOMETER
- FILTER
- DRY DOCK
- GRAVEL, DRIFTWOOD AND PLANTS
- WATER CONDITIONER
- FOOD
- CALCIUM AND VITAMIN POWDER
- AQUARIUM SIPHON
- FEEDING TUB

## FUN FACT

Turtles can breathe through their bottoms.
Turtles absorb oxygen from water through their butt, however, they still need to come to the surface to breathe air.

## BEN'S TOP TIP

The most demanding ongoing turtle task is the weekly water change. I made every Saturday morning 'turtle cleaning day'. If you do your water change at the same time every week, you won't forget and it will become part of your normal routine.

# GECKOS

**SPECIES:** Smooth knob-tailed gecko and thick-tailed gecko

**LIFESPAN:** 10+ years

**SIZE:** 10–15 cm

**MAINTENANCE LEVEL:** Low

**COST:** $$

Geckos are shy, nocturnal lizards, which means they are more active at night, when they come out in search of food. They are the perfect pet reptile if you have a busy lifestyle, as geckos don't require time-consuming maintenance and prefer not to be handled.

## HOUSING

Geckos can be housed on their own, or in a small group of 2–3 animals. I recommend a glass reptile enclosure measuring 60 x 45 x 45 cm to keep up to three adult geckos. Place a few small hides, artificial plants and a shallow water dish inside their enclosure. Use desert sand or coconut fibre (for thick-tailed geckos) on the floor of their enclosure to provide the perfect substrate (bedding) for your gecko to burrow and dig in.

## EQUIPMENT

Your geckos will need heat, but they don't tolerate very high temperatures. Put a reptile heat mat under one side of their enclosure to create a warm end. Temperatures at the warm end should be kept between 28 and 30 °C and 18 and 22 °C at the cooler end.

**YOU SHOULD NOT HANDLE YOUR GECKOS TOO OFTEN AS THEY STRESS EASILY AND THIS CAN CAUSE THEM TO DROP THEIR TAILS.**

• • • • • • • • • • • • • •

You will need a thermometer and thermostat to check and control these temperatures.

Give your gecko ultraviolet light (UV light) by placing a reptile UVB globe on top of the enclosure and running it for 12 hours each day.

## MAINTENANCE

Keep your gecko's enclosure clean by doing a daily check and removing any poo, shed skin or uneaten insects. Wash and replenish their water dish each day. Use a water sprayer to give your gecko's enclosure a light mist of water every second day. Replace the substrate completely every 2–3 months and clean the enclosure using a reptile disinfectant. You should not handle your geckos too often as they stress easily and this can cause them to drop their tails.

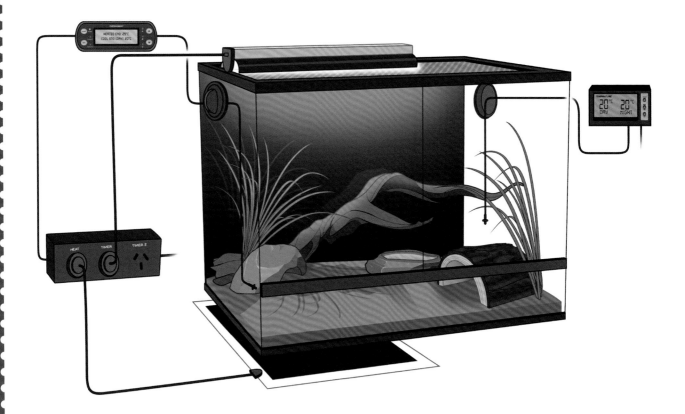

## DIET

Geckos are insectivores. Feed your lizards a range of nutritious live insects (crickets, wood roaches, black soldier fly larvae and silkworms). Make sure you dust live insects with a calcium and vitamin supplement before offering them to your geckos. Young geckos should be fed every day and adult geckos can be fed every second day.

**MAKE SURE YOU DUST LIVE INSECTS WITH A CALCIUM AND VITAMIN SUPPLEMENT BEFORE OFFERING THEM TO YOUR GECKOS.**

• • • • • • • • • • •

# CHECKLIST

- REPTILE ENCLOSURE
- HEAT MAT
- UVB GLOBE
- THERMOSTAT
- THERMOMETER
- HIDES
- WATER BOWL
- SUBSTRATE
- FOOD
- CALCIUM AND VITAMIN POWDER
- WATER SPRAYER
- REPTILE DISINFECTANT

## BEN'S TOP TIP

Geckos spend most of the day sleeping in their hide or burrow. Use a special purple LED light to view your geckos when they are active at night to replicate the moonlight.

## FUN FACT

Geckos lick their own eyeballs to keep them clean because most species lack eyelids.

# CREEPY CRAWLY PETS — CRITTERS

## STICK INSECTS

**SPECIES: Spiny leaf insect and goliath stick insect**

**LIFESPAN: 1–1.5 years**

**SIZE: 15–20 cm**

**MAINTENANCE LEVEL: Low**

**COST: $**

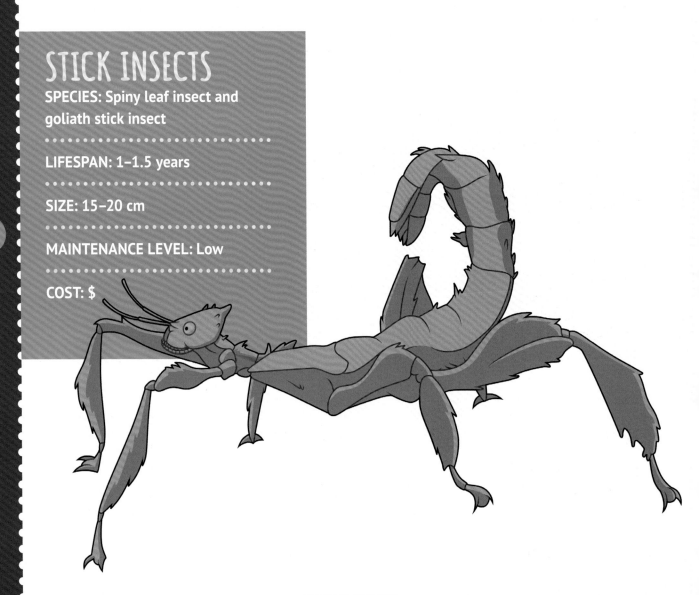

> ## STICK INSECTS ARE A LOW-COST, SUPER-EASY PET TO CARE FOR AND BREED AT HOME.

Stick insects, also known as phasmids, are the ultimate insect pet. You can share in their amazing journey starting from a tiny egg, watching them become nymphs (baby insects) and completing their life cycle by reaching adulthood. They are a low-cost, super-easy pet to care for and breed at home.

## HOUSING

Stick insects can be housed in a well-ventilated plastic, glass, or mesh enclosure. Make sure it is tall enough to fit branches of gum (eucalyptus) leaves and roomy enough for your insects to hang upside down to shed their skin. Find a well-lit room for their enclosure, but somewhere not so warm your insects will overheat.

## EQUIPMENT

Place a glass jar (with a lid) filled with water in the middle of the enclosure to hold the branches of gum leaves. Ask an adult to help you poke holes in the lid of the jar to insert the stems of the gum leaf branches. You need to keep the lid on the jar so your insects don't fall into the water and drown. You will also need to put a 1–2 cm layer of substrate (coconut fibre or peat moss) on the floor of their enclosure.

## MAINTENANCE

Give your stick insects a light mist of water once a day using a water sprayer. Mist both the gum leaves and the substrate to keep your stick insect's environment humid. If your stick insects get too dry they will have trouble shedding their skin. Completely replace their substrate every 2–3 months; but don't forget to sort through it to find hidden treasure – your stick insect's eggs!

## DIET

The only thing you need to feed your stick insects is fresh gum leaves. Put a few branches into the jar filled with water to stop the leaves from drying out. Replace the leaves every 4–7 days to make sure they are always fresh.

## CHECKLIST

- ENCLOSURE
- GLASS JAR WITH A LID
- SUBSTRATE
- WATER SPRAYER
- FRESH GUM LEAVES

### BEN'S TOP TIP

Stick insects are super easy to breed. When I was younger, I collected their eggs and bred hundreds of different stick insects to sell to my local pet store to make some pocket money.

### FUN FACT

Stick insects can clone themselves. Female stick insects can lay fertile eggs without a male. All their offspring are females and clones of their mum. This amazing ability is known as parthenogenesis.

# GIANT BURROWING COCKROACHES

**LIFESPAN:** 10+ years

........................................................

**SIZE:** 7.5 cm

........................................................

**MAINTENANCE LEVEL:** Low

........................................................

**COST:** $

Giant burrowing cockroaches are large, nocturnal insects native to north Queensland. They are seriously the coolest bugs and super easy to look after. Reassure any concerned adults in your life that giant burrowing cockroaches are very clean animals and don't carry diseases.

## HOUSING

Use a well-ventilated glass or plastic enclosure measuring 30 x 30 x 30 cm to house 2–3 adult roaches. Make sure the enclosure has a secure lid to stop your roaches from escaping and freaking out your mum.

## EQUIPMENT

Your giant burrowing cockroaches' enclosure should be kept at temperatures between 18 and 26 °C. You may need a heat mat to keep them warm in winter. Place the heat mat at the back of the enclosure (not underneath) to make sure you don't overheat your roaches, as they like to burrow down to the bottom of their enclosure. Check temperatures using a thermometer.

### REASSURE ANY CONCERNED ADULTS IN YOUR LIFE THAT GIANT BURROWING COCKROACHES ARE VERY CLEAN ANIMALS AND DON'T CARRY DISEASES.

These roaches live in deep burrows in the wild. You can create a natural environment for them by filling the bottom of their enclosure with 5–10 cm of sandy soil. Mixing sand with coconut fibre or peat moss provides the perfect substrate for your roaches to happily burrow in.

101

## MAINTENANCE

Lightly mist the substrate in your roaches' enclosure with a water sprayer 2–3 times a week to keep it damp (not wet). Be careful not to over-spray and soak everything as too much water can make them sick. You will only need to completely replace their substrate every 4 or 5 months.

## DIET

Feed your giant burrowing cockroaches dead, dry gum (eucalyptus) leaves. Just spread a layer of dry gum leaves across the surface of their soil and add new dead leaves every few weeks. Your roaches will also enjoy pieces of chopped apple, banana or carrot that you can offer them twice a week.

**FEED YOUR GIANT BURROWING COCKROACHES DEAD, DRY GUM LEAVES.**

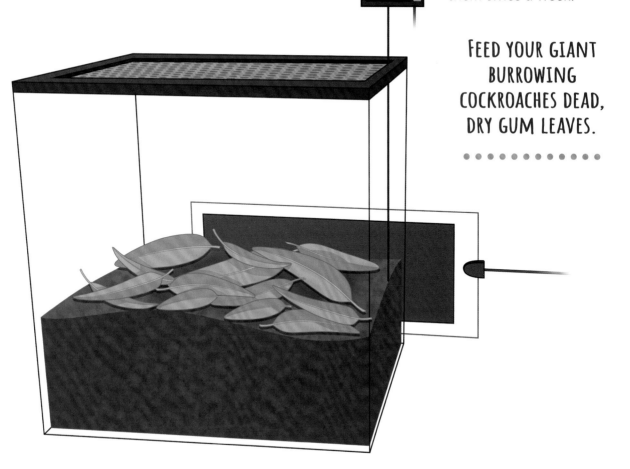

## CHECKLIST

- ENCLOSURE
- HEAT MAT
- THERMOMETER
- SUBSTRATE
- WATER SPRAYER
- DRY GUM LEAVES

## BEN'S TOP TIP

Always sit down when you are handling your giant cockroach. These insects are so large and heavy that if you accidentally drop them from a standing height they can get seriously injured.

## FUN FACT

Giant burrowing cockroaches are the heaviest roach in the world. Adults weigh up to 30 grams.

# SCORPIONS

**SPECIES:** Flinders Range scorpion and black rock scorpion

**LIFESPAN:** 6–10 years

**SIZE:** 5–12 cm

**MAINTENANCE LEVEL:** Low

**COST:** $

Scorpions are nocturnal arachnids (have eight legs) that are closely related to spiders. They are a unique pet and if you look carefully you can watch them scurrying around their enclosure at night in search of food.

CAUTION: ALL SCORPIONS CAN GIVE A PAINFUL STING. IF YOU ARE ALLERGIC TO BEE STINGS, I STRONGLY ADVISE THAT YOU DO NOT KEEP A SCORPION AS A PET. IT IS VERY IMPORTANT THAT YOU NEVER TRY TO TOUCH OR HOLD YOUR SCORPION.

## HOUSING

Most scorpions are best housed on their own in a small-to-medium sized glass or plastic enclosure measuring 30 x 30 x 30 cm (minimum).

Make sure the enclosure has a secure lid and some ventilation (but not too much).

## EQUIPMENT

Your scorpion's enclosure should be kept at temperatures between 18 and 26 °C. You may need a heat mat to keep them warm in winter. Place the heat mat to one side underneath the enclosure, so your scorpion's enclosure has a warm end and a cooler end. Check temperatures with a thermometer.

Scorpions live in burrows or underneath rocks and logs in the wild. To create a natural environment, fill the base of their enclosure with 5–10 cm of sandy soil. Mixing sand with coconut fibre or peat moss provides the perfect substrate for the scorpions to burrow in. Place some flat pieces of bark in the enclosure for them to hide under.

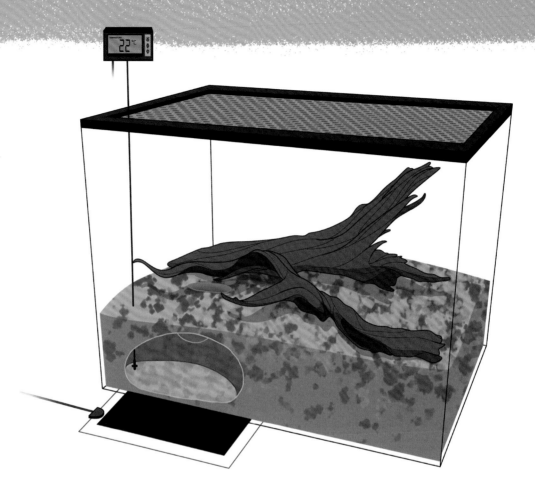

## MAINTENANCE

Clean your scorpion's enclosure regularly by removing any dead or uneaten insects. Lightly mist the substrate with a water sprayer 2–3 times a week to keep it damp. Scorpions absorb moisture from their surroundings so it is very important not to let the substrate dry out. Completely replace the substrate every 4–5 months.

## DIET

Scorpions are insectivores. Feed your scorpion once a week on a variety of live insects (crickets, wood roaches and silkworms). Take care and always offer food to your scorpion using a long set of tweezers.

**ALWAYS OFFER FOOD TO YOUR SCORPION USING A LONG SET OF TWEEZERS**

• • • • • • • • • • •

# CHECKLIST

- ENCLOSURE
- HEAT MAT
- THERMOMETER
- SUBSTRATE
- HIDE
- WATER SPRAYER
- FOOD
- TWEEZERS

## BEN'S TOP TIP

You can purchase a UV black light and go searching for wild scorpions at night. When I was in the jungles of Borneo I found the BIGGEST scorpion I've ever seen. It was larger than my entire hand!

## FUN FACT

Scorpions glow in the dark. Due to fluorescent chemicals in a scorpion's exoskeleton they glow bright green at night under a UV black light.

# HERMIT CRABS

**SPECIES:** Australian land hermit crab

............................................

**LIFESPAN:** 10–15 years

............................................

**SIZE:** 2–6 cm

............................................

**MAINTENANCE LEVEL:** Medium

............................................

**COST:** $$

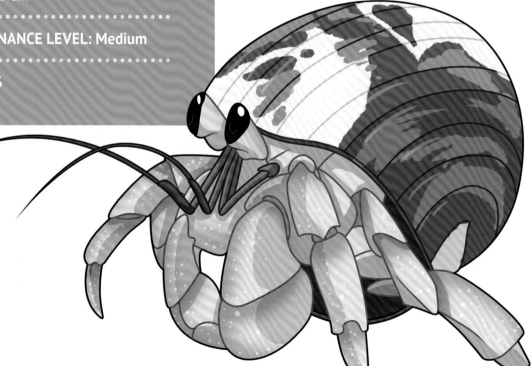

Hermit crabs can be found in the northern, warmer parts of Australia. They make cute, compact pets and their busy daily activities (burrowing, climbing, swimming, swapping shells) are fun to watch. Hermit crabs also tolerate being handled gently for short periods. There is quite a bit of work involved in looking after hermit crabs properly, so make sure you are fully prepared to become a crab carer. It's well worth the effort.

## HOUSING

Hermit crabs are very social and should be kept in small groups. Use a glass enclosure measuring 30 x 30 x 30 cm (minimum) to house 2–4 small hermit crabs. Bigger crabs should be kept in a larger enclosure. A glass lid works best for keeping their environment humid.

## EQUIPMENT

The temperature in your hermit crabs' enclosure should be kept between 24 and 30 °C. You will need a heat mat to keep them warm. Place the heat mat to one side underneath the enclosure so that the crabs have a warm end and a cool end. Check temperatures using a thermometer. Hermit crabs also require high humidity (moisture in the air) to breathe. The humidity in their enclosure should be kept between 75 and 90% and checked using a hygrometer.

Hermit crabs love to burrow and need to dig underground when they go through a moult (shed their skin to grow). To create a natural environment, fill the base of the enclosure with 10–15 cm of sandy soil. Mixing sand with coconut fibre or peat moss provides the perfect substrate for the crabs to burrow in.

Hermit crabs also need fresh and salt water, places to hide and branches to climb. Fresh water must be treated with a water conditioner and water bowls should be deep enough for your crabs to swim in, but still climb out of easily. Sea salt can be added to tap water to make salt water. You will also need to provide some larger spare shells for your crabs to move into as they grow.

> HERMIT CRABS ARE VERY SOCIAL AND SHOULD BE KEPT IN SMALL GROUPS.

109

## MAINTENANCE

Remove any uneaten food and replace your hermit crabs' fresh and salt water every day. Lightly mist the substrate with a water sprayer at least 2–3 times a week to keep it damp. Make sure their enclosure never dries out, as this will make your crabs sick. Completely replace their substrate every 2–3 months.

## DIET

Hermit crabs are omnivores. You need to feed your crabs a variety of foods. A dry hermit crab mix should always be available in their feed dish. You should also offer fresh fruits and vegetables (apple, carrot and leafy greens) 2–3 times each week. For an occasional treat hermit crabs love small pieces of meat (chicken and fish). Add a cuttlebone as an extra source of calcium.

**MAKE SURE THEIR ENCLOSURE NEVER DRIES OUT, AS THIS WILL MAKE YOUR CRABS SICK.**

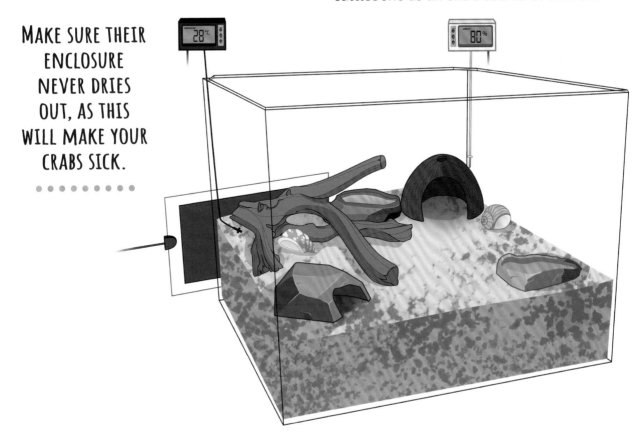

## CHECKLIST

- GLASS ENCLOSURE
- HEAT MAT
- THERMOMETER
- HYGROMETER
- SUBSTRATE
- HIDE AND BRANCHES
- WATER SPRAYER
- WATER BOWLS
- FOOD BOWL
- SEA SALT
- WATER CONDITIONER
- FOOD
- SPARE SHELLS

### BEN'S TOP TIP

Hermit crabs are great escape artists. Make sure you have a secure lid on their enclosure. Once, when my family and I went away on holidays my grandmother forgot to close the lid and my crabs all escaped. When I got home we found they had climbed up and were hiding in the curtains.

### FUN FACT

Hermit crabs breed in the ocean. Although adult hermit crabs live on land, females move into the sea to lay their eggs. Baby hermit crabs will live in the ocean as larvae before developing into crabs and coming onto the land.

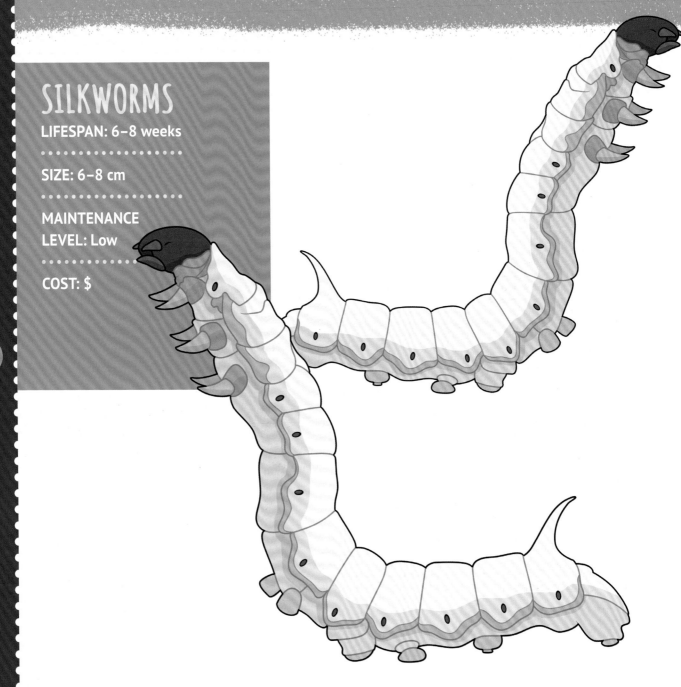

# SILKWORMS

**LIFESPAN:** 6–8 weeks

**SIZE:** 6–8 cm

**MAINTENANCE LEVEL:** Low

**COST:** $

The lifecycle of a silkworm is short but amazing to watch. Starting from a tiny egg the silkworms begin to grow and after about four weeks they spin a silk cocoon. A couple of weeks later little moths wriggle their way out of the cocoon and start laying tiny eggs to begin the lifecycle all over again. The most important thing you need to care for silkworms is access to truckloads of fresh mulberry leaves.

## HOUSING

You need a cool, dry, environment to raise silkworms. A small well-ventilated plastic enclosure with lots of little holes in the lid is perfect. Make sure you keep their enclosure away from windows so

**SILKWORMS ARE SUPER EASY TO LOOK AFTER.**

your silkworms don't overheat. Remember, silkworms are very delicate, sensitive creatures. Never let anyone spray potentially harmful aerosols with chemicals around them.

## EQUIPMENT

Silkworms are super easy to look after. You barely need any equipment at all. Just put a sheet of paper towel on the base of their enclosure to help absorb any excess moisture.

## MAINTENANCE

Clean your silkworms' enclosure every day by removing their poo and any uneaten or dry leaves. Replace the sheet of paper towel. By completing these two simple tasks you will keep your silkworms' enclosure dry.

113

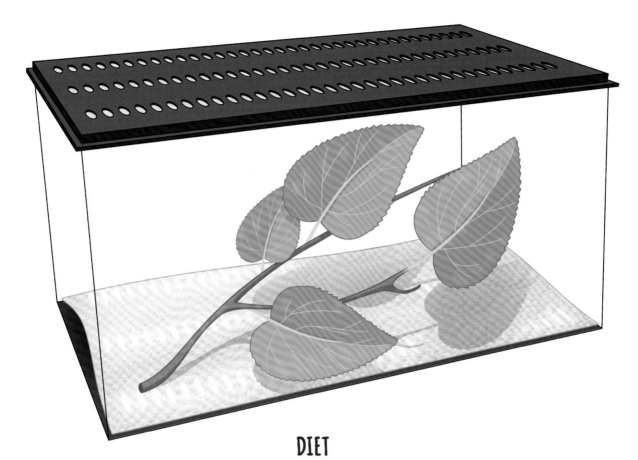

**BECAUSE SILKWORMS GROW RAPIDLY THEY GET VERY HUNGRY.**

● ● ● ● ● ● ● ● ●

## DIET

Because silkworms grow rapidly they get very hungry. Feed your silkworms on fresh mulberry leaves, adding new leaves 2–3 times a day. Silkworms can also be fed on a special 'silkworm chow' diet that can be purchased from some pet stores or online.

## CHECKLIST

- ENCLOSURE
- PAPER TOWEL
- MULBERRY LEAVES
- SILKWORM CHOW (OPTIONAL)

## BEN'S TOP TIP

Your neighbours will usually get upset if you start pinching their mulberry leaves without permission. Always go and ask politely if they would allow you to use their tree to feed your silkworms.

## FUN FACT

A silkworm's cocoon is made from a single thread of silk. This single thread of silk can be up to 900 metres long.

## WORM FARM

**SPECIES:** Compost worms

.....................................

**LIFESPAN:** 4–6 years

.....................................

**SIZE:** 4–8 cm

.....................................

**MAINTENANCE LEVEL:** Low

.....................................

**COST:** $

Worms are the perfect pet for helping you and your family care for our planet. Not only do worms reduce your household waste by composting food scraps, they also provide you with fabulous free fertiliser for the garden. Adults will love the idea of bringing compost worms into the family.

## HOUSING

I recommend you buy a purpose-built worm farm at a nursery, from a hardware store, or online. Check with your local council first, as some councils provide free worm farms to residents. These worm farms are set up with everything you need to raise worms and harvest compost. Position your worm farm in a warm spot that does not get too hot in summer, or too cold in winter.

Worm farms usually have three layers. Each layer is made up of a tray with holes in it to allow your worms to move between layers.

**CHECK WITH YOUR LOCAL COUNCIL FIRST, AS SOME COUNCILS PROVIDE FREE WORM FARMS TO RESIDENTS.**

The top layer is where organic matter (food scraps) is placed for the worms to feed on, the middle layer is where the worms live and the bottom layer is where the worms' waste is collected.

## EQUIPMENT

Follow the instructions to assemble your kit and put damp compost mix in the worms' living tray. Place a few sheets of wet newspaper over the top to help keep it damp. A colony of compost worms can then be introduced to the compost mix.

Put organic matter (food scraps) in the top feeding tray and cover them with a piece of hessian or a 'worm blanket'. Your worms will happily feed on these scraps and begin to breed. They will also produce 'worm wee' which collects in the lower waste layer and can be drained from a tap into a bucket. Worm wee is full of nutrients and is great for fertilising your garden plants.

117

## MAINTENANCE

Your worms need a dark, damp environment to thrive. Keep your worm farm moist by pouring a little fresh water over the top layer once a week. Drain any excess liquid from the bottom waste layer into a bucket and use it to water plants.

## DIET

Feed your compost worms on a variety of organic waste. They will enjoy fruit and veggie scraps, crushed eggshells, bread crusts and pasta. Never feed your worms any citrus fruit (orange or lemon skins), onions, garlic or meat. When you are trying to establish your worm farm don't overfeed your worms as uneaten food scraps will begin to rot and smell.

**KEEP YOUR WORM FARM MOIST BY POURING A LITTLE FRESH WATER OVER THE TOP LAYER ONCE A WEEK.**

118

## CHECKLIST

- WORM FARM KIT
- COMPOST MIX
- NEWSPAPER
- HESSIAN
- COMPOST WORMS
- BUCKET
- ORGANIC WASTE

## FUN FACT

A compost worm can eat its own weight in food in a single day.

## BEN'S TOP TIP

When I add organic matter to my worm farm I put the food waste on one half of the feeding tray. I check my worms have eaten this before adding more food, this time to the other side. Using this system makes it easy for me to avoid overfeeding my worms. Pet worms are winners for people and the planet.

# WET PETS – FISH AND AMPHIBIANS

## SIAMESE FIGHTING FISH

**SPECIES:** Also known as bettas

**LIFESPAN:** 3–5 years

**SIZE:** 7 cm

**MAINTENANCE LEVEL:** Low

**COST:** $

If you love the idea of caring for a fish but you don't have the space, time or interest in maintaining a huge tank, then a fighting fish might be the perfect 'wet pet' for you.

## HOUSING

A small 15–20-litre fish tank with a glass or plastic lid is the ideal enclosure for you to house one adult Siamese fighting fish. Make sure you keep males on their own, because if you put boys together they will fight (they are called fighting fish for a reason!). Set up and run your new tank with water for at least a week before getting your fish. Add some bio culture (good bacteria) to the water every day during the set-up week.

## EQUIPMENT

Siamese fighting fish are a tropical species that need water temperatures between 24 and 26 °C. Use an aquarium water heater to achieve this and regularly check the temperature of your tank using a thermometer. You need a small filter to help keep the tank clean. Make sure the filter is not too powerful as your fighting fish prefer a tank with minimal water flow.

**DECORATE YOUR TANK WITH SMOOTH AQUARIUM GRAVEL AND LIVE OR ARTIFICIAL SILK PLANTS FOR YOUR FISH TO HIDE IN.**

Decorate your tank with smooth aquarium gravel and live or artificial silk plants for your fish to hide in.

## MAINTENANCE

To keep your Siamese fighting fish's tank clean you will need to change a small amount of their water once a week. Use an aquarium siphon to carefully drain the tank by 15–20% and vacuum any poo or uneaten food from the gravel.

Never put fresh water from the tap directly into your tank without treating it, or you might kill your fish. Prepare the water first by putting it in a clean bucket and adding water conditioner to remove chlorine and any other harmful chemicals. After you top up the tank check the pH of the water using a freshwater test kit. The pH should be 7.0–7.5.

## DIET

Feed your fish a small pinch of Siamese fighting fish pellets or granules once a day. Don't overfeed your fish, as leftover food will make the water get dirty very quickly. Your fighting fish will also enjoy live bloodworms and brine shrimp as a treat 1–2 times a week.

**DON'T OVERFEED YOUR FISH, AS LEFTOVER FOOD WILL MAKE THE WATER GET DIRTY VERY QUICKLY.**

122

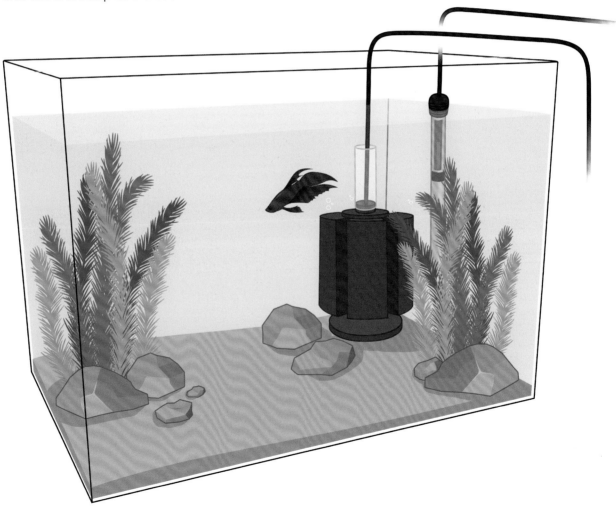

# CHECKLIST

- FISH TANK
- AQUARIUM WATER HEATER
- THERMOMETER
- FILTER
- AQUARIUM SIPHON
- AQUARIUM GRAVEL
- PLANTS
- FOOD
- WATER CONDITIONER
- BIO CULTURE
- FRESHWATER TEST KIT

## BEN'S TOP TIP

If you see lots of bubbles forming in a corner of your fighting fish's tank, don't stress. Male fighting fish create 'bubble nests'. In the wild, a female fighting fish will come and lay her eggs in the nest. The male will then protect the nest and babies when they hatch.

## FUN FACT

Siamese fighting fish can breathe air like us. They have a specialised breathing system (called a labyrinth organ) that lets them take oxygen from the water's surface.

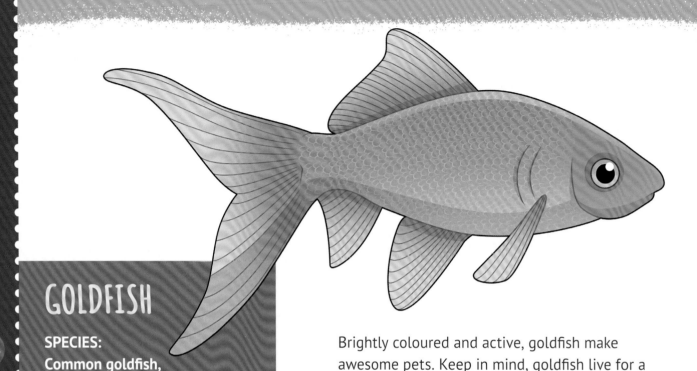

# GOLDFISH

**SPECIES:**
**Common goldfish,**
**comets and fantails**

**LIFESPAN: 10–15**
**years**

**SIZE: 20 cm+**

**MAINTENANCE**
**LEVEL: High**

**COST: $$**

Brightly coloured and active, goldfish make awesome pets. Keep in mind, goldfish live for a long time and grow very big. This means you will need space for a large tank and time to dedicate each week to cleaning and maintaining your goldfish tank.

## HOUSING

Use an 80–100 litre fish tank with a glass or plastic lid to house 4–6 goldfish. Since goldfish can grow very large, small bowls and tanks are not suitable enclosures for them. Set up and run your new tank for at least a week before getting your goldfish. Add some bio culture (good bacteria) to the water every day during the set-up week.

## EQUIPMENT

Goldfish are a cold-water species and prefer a water temperature of 20–24 °C. Regularly check the temperature of your tank using a thermometer. Be careful not to position the tank in direct sunlight or you might overheat your goldfish in summer.

You need a powerful filter to help keep the tank clean. Make sure the water flow of the filter can be adjusted so the current is not too strong for fancier goldfish varieties like fantails. You also need to put an LED light on top of the tank and run it for 6–8 hours each day.

Decorate your tank with smooth aquarium gravel and live or artificial silk plants for your fish to hide in. Add pieces of driftwood and other aquarium-safe ornaments.

## MAINTENANCE

Goldfish are poo-machines so you will need to change some of their water every week. Use an aquarium siphon to carefully drain the tank by 20–25% and vacuum any poo or uneaten food from the gravel.

**GOLDFISH LIVE FOR A LONG TIME AND GROW VERY BIG.**

Never put fresh water from the tap directly into your tank without treating it or you might kill your goldfish. Prepare the water first by putting it in a clean bucket and adding water conditioner to remove chlorine and any other harmful chemicals. After you top up your tank check the pH of the water using a freshwater test kit. The pH should be 6.5–7.5. Aquarium salt can also be added when changing the water as it is beneficial for gill function and disease prevention.

22°C

## DIET

Feed goldfish flakes or granules to your fish once a day. Offer your fish only as much food as they can eat in under one minute. Don't overfeed them as leftover food will make the water get dirty very quickly. Your goldfish will also enjoy live bloodworms and brine shrimp as a treat and will eat live aquarium plants and some leafy vegetables such as kale or spinach.

OFFER YOUR FISH ONLY AS MUCH FOOD AS THEY CAN EAT IN UNDER ONE MINUTE.

• • • • • • • • •

—WET PETS—

# CHECKLIST

- FISH TANK
- FILTER
- THERMOMETER
- AQUARIUM SIPHON
- LED LIGHT
- AQUARIUM GRAVEL
- PLANTS
- DRIFTWOOD
- FOOD
- WATER CONDITIONER
- BIO CULTURE
- FRESHWATER TEST KIT
- AQUARIUM SALT

## FUN FACT

Goldfish have been kept as pets for over 2000 years. They were first domesticated by the Chinese who considered them a symbol of good luck.

## BEN'S TOP TIP

Despite the name, 'goldfish bowls' do not make suitable homes for goldfish. For a healthy and happy life, provide your goldfish with a spacious tank that has lots of hiding places and a powerful filter to keep the water clean.

# TROPICAL FISH

**SPECIES: Tetras, guppies, mollies, platies, catfish and many more**

**LIFESPAN: 5–10 years**

**SIZE: 5 cm+**

**MAINTENANCE LEVEL: High**

**COST: $$**

Tropical fish are gorgeous and come in many shapes, sizes and colours. Setting up a community tank with different species is very rewarding. If you're prepared to invest the time in maintaining a tropical tank, you will have happy, healthy fish. Watching your tropical fish will become a relaxing activity to de-stress the whole family.

## HOUSING

Like tropical fish, fish tanks come in many different shapes and sizes. Consider the space you have available and the species and number of fish you would like to keep when choosing the size of your tank. As a guide, use an 80–100-litre fish tank with a glass lid to house 30–40

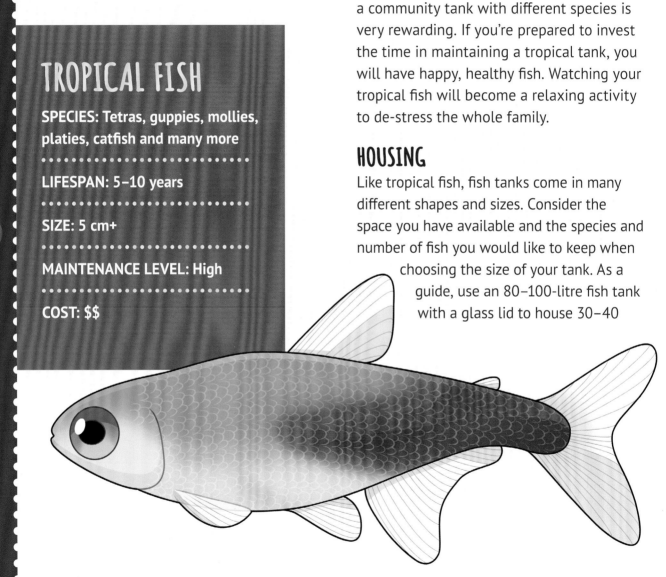

small tropical fish. Set up and run your new tropical tank for at least a week before getting your fish. Add some bio culture (good bacteria) to the water every day during the set-up week.

Many tropical fish can be kept in a community aquarium housing different species. Check that the species you are planning to mix are not aggressive towards one another. If you take good care of your tank and provide plenty of plant cover, many tropical fish will happily breed in captivity.

## EQUIPMENT

Tropical fish need water temperatures between 24 and 28 °C. Use an aquarium water heater to achieve this and regularly check the temperature of your tank using a thermometer. Be careful not to position your tank in direct sunlight as this can encourage algae to grow.

You need a powerful filter to help keep the tank clean. External canister filters are the most effective and require less maintenance than smaller filters that sit inside the tank. Make sure the water flow of the filter can be adjusted so that the current is not too strong. Use an aerator to help put oxygen into the water. You also need to place an LED light on top of the tank and run it for 6–8 hours each day.

Decorate your tank with smooth aquarium gravel and live or artificial silk plants for your fish to hide in. Add pieces of driftwood and other aquarium-safe ornaments.

## MAINTENANCE

You will need to change some of the water in your tank once a week. Use an aquarium siphon to carefully drain the tank by 20–25% and vacuum any poo or uneaten food from the gravel.

Never put fresh water from the tap directly into your tank without treating it or you might kill your fish. Prepare the water first by putting it in a clean bucket and adding water conditioner to remove chlorine and any other harmful chemicals. After you top up the tank check the pH of the water using a freshwater test kit. The pH should be 6.5–7.5. Aquarium salt can also be added when changing the water as it is beneficial for gill function and disease prevention.

## DIET

Feed tropical fish flakes or pellets to your fish once a day. Offer your fish only as much food as they can eat in under one minute. Don't overfeed them as leftover food will make the water get dirty very quickly. Your tropical fish will also enjoy live bloodworms and brine shrimp as a treat 1–2 times a week and will eat live aquarium plants.

**NEVER PUT FRESH WATER FROM THE TAP DIRECTLY INTO YOUR TANK WITHOUT TREATING IT OR YOU MIGHT KILL YOUR FISH.**

## CHECKLIST

- FISH TANK
- CANISTER FILTER
- AQUARIUM WATER HEATER
- THERMOMETER
- LED LIGHT
- AQUARIUM SIPHON
- GRAVEL
- PLANTS
- DRIFTWOOD
- FOOD
- WATER CONDITIONER
- BIO CULTURE
- FRESHWATER TEST KIT
- AQUARIUM SALT

### BEN'S TOP TIP
If your fish have babies, make sure you separate the fry (baby fish) into a separate tank or put them in a mesh rearing container floating inside the tank, or larger fish might eat them.

### FUN FACT
Some tropical fish lay eggs, while others give birth to live young.

# AXOLOTLS

**SPECIES: Also known as the Mexican walking fish**

.......................................

**LIFESPAN: 10–12 years**

.......................................

**SIZE: 15–25 cm**

.......................................

**MAINTENANCE LEVEL: Medium**

.......................................

**COST: $$**

Axolotls are the weirdest looking wet pet you'll ever find. They are amphibians who live their lives in water and are the larval (baby) stage of a salamander. Axolotls are amazing, but also very messy wet pets, so be prepared to do plenty of tank cleaning.

## HOUSING

Use a fish tank measuring at least 60 x 45 x 45 cm to house one adult axolotl. Set up and run your new axolotl tank for at least a week before introducing your axolotl. Add some bio culture (good bacteria) to the water every day during the set-up week.

Axolotls are solitary creatures and happily live on their own. If you decide to care for more than one, you will need a larger fish tank with plenty of hiding places for them to retreat and feel safe. Don't keep two males together. Your axolotls will not like high temperatures, so keep their tank away from windows and direct sunlight.

## EQUIPMENT

Axolotls are a cold-water species and prefer water temperatures between 14 and 20 °C. Regularly check the temperature of your tank using a thermometer.

Axolotls make a mighty mess. You need a powerful filter to help keep the tank clean. Make sure the water flow of the filter can be adjusted so that the current is not too strong. Use an aerator to help put oxygen into the water. You also need to place an LED light on top of the tank and run it for 6–8 hours each day.

**AXOLOTLS ARE THE WEIRDEST LOOKING WET PET YOU'LL EVER FIND.**

Axolotls will eat any small object they can fit in their mouths. Keep the bottom of the tank bare for easy cleaning. Alternatively, use fine sand or course river pebbles that they can't swallow on the bottom of their tank. Add smooth driftwood and live and artificial plants.

## MAINTENANCE

You will need to change some of the water in the tank once a week. Use an aquarium siphon to carefully drain the tank by 20–25% and vacuum any poo or uneaten food from the sand or pebbles.

Never put fresh water from the tap directly into your tank without treating it or you might kill your axolotl. Prepare the water first by putting it in a clean bucket and adding water conditioner to remove chlorine and any other harmful chemicals. After you top up the tank check the pH of the water using a freshwater test kit. The pH should be 7.0–7.5.

**FEED YOUR AXOLOTL A VARIETY OF LIVE FOODS.**

## DIET

Axolotls are carnivores. Feed your axolotl a variety of live foods (crickets, wood roaches, earthworms, silkworms and black worms). You can also offer pelleted diets as a supplement. When your axolotls are young feed them once a day and after they are fully grown every second day.

## CHECKLIST

- FISH TANK
- FILTER
- AERATOR
- THERMOMETER
- LED LIGHT
- AQUARIUM SIPHON
- FINE SAND OR COURSE RIVER PEBBLES
- PLANTS
- DRIFTWOOD
- FOOD
- LONG TWEEZERS
- WATER CONDITIONER
- BIO CULTURE
- FRESHWATER TEST KIT

### BEN'S TOP TIP
Use long tweezers to offer food to your axolotls so there is no uneaten food left in the tank.

### FUN FACT
Axolotls can re-grow body parts.
Axolotls have the amazing ability to re-grow damaged body parts and can even replace a lost leg.

# FROGS

**SPECIES:** Green tree frogs
. . . . . . . . . . . . . . . . . . . . . . . .

**LIFESPAN:** 20 years+
. . . . . . . . . . . . . . . . . . . . . . . .

**SIZE:** 10–12 cm
. . . . . . . . . . . . . . . . . . . . . . . .

**MAINTENANCE LEVEL:**
Medium
. . . . . . . . . . . . . . . . . . . . . . . .

**COST:** $$

Frogs are one of my favourite 'alternative pets'. I have a frog tank in my living room and spend more time watching them than the TV. Frogs are such cool little characters. Their bouncing, climbing and splashing about always keeps me entertained.

## HOUSING

Use a glass reptile enclosure to house your frogs because they are waterproof, well-ventilated and secure. An enclosure measuring 60 x 45 x 60 cm will comfortably suit one or two adult green tree frogs. Frogs are great escape artists, so check the doors of the enclosure lock and there are no small gaps. If you plan to keep more than one frog, they need to be about the same size because larger frogs often try and eat smaller ones.

## EQUIPMENT

Frogs are amphibians, and like reptiles they are ectotherms and rely on the environment to control their body temperature. You need to provide them with a source of heat.

Place a ceramic heat emitter above the mesh lid at one end of their enclosure. Use a thermostat to control the temperature of the heat emitter and set it at 28–30 °C. Your frogs need a warm end and a cool end so they can move towards the warmth if they are cold, or away from the heat if they become too hot. The cool end should be kept between 22 and 24 °C.

Frogs also need sunlight (ultraviolet light) for healthy growth and development. A reptile UVB tube should be placed on top of the enclosure and run for 12 hours each day.

Green tree frogs love to climb, so give your frogs plenty of branches and even a rock background with ledges to sit on. Add artificial plants, log hides and a large water bowl. Cover the bottom of their enclosure with coconut fibre.

> **FROGS NEED SUNLIGHT (ULTRAVIOLET LIGHT) FOR HEALTHY GROWTH AND DEVELOPMENT.**

## MAINTENANCE

Your frogs need a damp environment. Mist their enclosure (including the coconut fibre) with water every day using a water sprayer. Regularly check and clean up any poo or uneaten food. Completely replace the coconut fibre every 6–8 weeks.

It is very important that you don't handle your frogs too often. They have very delicate skin and can absorb chemicals from your hands which can be dangerous to them. When you need to move your frog for cleaning or feeding make sure your hands are clean and wet.

Wash, rinse and refresh your frog's water bowl every day. Add water conditioner to any new tap water to remove chlorine and other harmful chemicals before putting it in their water bowl.

Never use fly sprays or perfumes in the same room as your frogs as this could make them sick, or worse.

**NEVER USE FLY SPRAYS OR PERFUMES IN THE SAME ROOM AS YOUR FROGS AS THIS COULD MAKE THEM SICK, OR WORSE.**

● ● ● ● ● ● ● ● ● ● ●

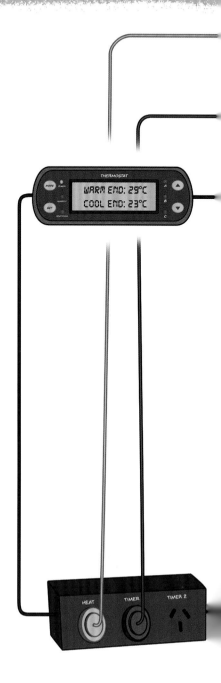

## DIET

Green tree frogs are insectivores. Feed them a variety of live insects (crickets, wood roaches, silkworms and black soldier fly larvae). Coat live insects in a calcium and vitamin powder before offering them to your frogs.

While your frogs are young feed them 1–2 times a day. Once they are fully grown you can feed them 2–3 times each week. Offer your adult frogs a defrosted pinkie mouse once a month as a treat. Use feeding tongs to feed your frogs individually, or place them into a separate feeding tub so that any uneaten insects do not escape and hide inside your frog's enclosure.

## BEN'S TOP TIP

Frogs play a critical role in the health of our waterways. Many frog species can only be found in Australia and some are endangered. You should never remove frogs or tadpoles from the wild.

## FUN FACT

Frogs can drink and breathe through their skin. Frogs have very special skin that can absorb water and oxygen from their surroundings.

## CHECKLIST

- GLASS REPTILE ENCLOSURE
- CERAMIC HEAT EMITTER
- REPTILE UVB TUBE
- THERMOSTAT
- CLIMBING BRANCHES
- HIDES
- ROCK BACKGROUND WITH LEDGES
- WATER SPRAYER
- WATER BOWL
- WATER CONDITIONER
- ARTIFICIAL PLANTS
- COCONUT FIBRE
- FOOD
- CALCIUM AND VITAMIN POWDER
- FEEDING TONGS
- FEEDING TUB

# FEATHERED PETS – BIRDS

STIMULATE
YOUR BUDGIES
BY PROVIDING A
VARIETY OF TOYS.

## BUDGIES

**SPECIES:** Budgerigar

**LIFESPAN:** 7–10 years

**SIZE:** 18–20 cm

**MAINTENANCE LEVEL:** Medium

**COST:** $$

Budgies are small, outgoing birds with big personalities. Being parakeets (small parrots), budgies are super smart. You can teach a budgie to talk and do tricks. Budgies love interacting with people and make great pets if you have the time to spend with them and the space to give them plenty of exercise.

## HOUSING

House your budgie in a high-quality wire bird enclosure measuring at least 50 x 40 x 65 cm (the bigger the better). Ideally, a powder-coated or stainless-steel enclosure is safest as the paint on some enclosures can make your budgie sick if they chew on it.

Some bird enclosures have tops that open, which are ideal for letting your budgie come in and out to interact with the family. Make sure your budgie has plenty of room to stretch out, fly between branches and climb. Position their enclosure against a wall, or in a corner away from any draughts. Cover your budgie's enclosure at night so they are not disturbed by noise and light. Line the tray at the bottom of your budgie's enclosure with shell grit or newspaper to collect waste.

Budgies can be housed alone, but they prefer the company of other budgies. If you have the space why not consider an outdoor flight aviary for a pair of budgies, or more.

## EQUIPMENT

A variety of natural branches and perches should be securely positioned at different heights in your budgies' enclosure. Branches of different thicknesses provide good exercise for your budgies' feet and help to keep their nails filed down.

Your budgies need food and water bowls for their dry food, fruits and veggies and fresh water. Budgies also love to take baths, so make sure you give your bird both a drinking bowl and a shallow bath.

Stimulate your budgies by providing a variety of toys. Change these toys regularly to keep your budgies entertained. Avoid toys made from rope or string as these materials can cause blockages in your budgies' gut if swallowed. Native flowers and leaves (eucalyptus, grevillea and bottlebrush) provide a great source of natural enrichment.

## FEED YOUR BUDGIES A FRESH, VARIED DIET EVERY DAY.

## MAINTENANCE

Wash, rinse and refresh your budgies' food and water bowls every day. Regularly check and clean branches and toys to remove any poo. Replace the newspaper or shell grit in the bottom tray every few days. Don't forget to use a bird-safe disinfectant when cleaning. Worm your budgies every three months by placing a worming solution in their drinking water.

## DIET

Feed your budgies a fresh, varied diet every day. Your feathered friends needs a budgie pellet or crumble, a good quality budgie seed mix and fresh vegetables and fruits (carrot, corn, beans, peas, spinach and apple). Millet sprays and unsalted nuts can also be offered as a treat once or twice a week.

Cuttlebone or a bowl of shell grit for calcium and vitamin D3 supplements in their drinking water a few times each week are also beneficial.

144

## CHECKLIST

- BIRD ENCLOSURE
- NATURAL PERCHES
- SHELL GRIT OR NEWSPAPER
- FOOD AND WATER BOWLS
- SHALLOW BATH
- TOYS
- BIRD-SAFE DISINFECTANT
- FOOD
- CALCIUM AND VITAMIN D3 SUPPLEMENTS
- WORMING SOLUTION

## BEN'S TOP TIP

To teach your budgie to talk, use repetition. Spend 10 minutes each morning and evening slowly repeating a word or short phrase. If your budgie begins to mimic you, reward them straight away with a special treat.

## FUN FACT

Budgies are the most commonly kept pet bird in the world.

# COCKATIELS

**SPECIES:** Cockatiel
(or quarrion)

.........................................

**LIFESPAN:** 15–25 years

.........................................

**SIZE:** 30–33 cm

.........................................

**MAINTENANCE LEVEL:** Medium

.........................................

**COST:** $$

Smart, cheeky and affectionate are three words that perfectly describe cockatiels. They make amazing companions. Cockatiels love nothing more than a good head scratch. You can spend hours stroking and playing with them every day. You can also train your cockatiel to do tricks like whistling tunes and mimicking speech.

## HOUSING

House your cockatiel in a high-quality wire bird enclosure measuring at least 80 x 50 x 80 cm high (the bigger the better). Ideally, a powder-coated or stainless-steel enclosure is safest as the paint on some enclosures can make your cockatiel sick if they chew on it. Provide your cockatiel with plenty of room to stretch out, fly between branches and climb.

Position their enclosure against a wall or in a corner away from draughts. Cover your cockatiel's enclosure at night so they are not disturbed by noise and light. Line the tray in the bottom of your cockatiel's enclosure with shell grit or newspaper to collect waste.

## EQUIPMENT

A variety of natural branches and perches should be securely positioned at different heights in your cockatiel's enclosure. Branches that have different thicknesses provide good exercise for your cockatiel's feet and help keep their nails filed down.

**COCKATIELS LOVE NOTHING MORE THAN A GOOD HEAD SCRATCH.**

Your cockatiel needs food and water bowls for their dry food, fruits and veggies and fresh water. Be careful not to position their perches over food and water bowls.

Stimulate your cockatiel by providing a variety of toys. Change these toys regularly to keep your cockatiel entertained. Avoid toys made from rope or string as these materials can cause blockages in your cockatiel's gut if swallowed. Native flowers and leaves (eucalyptus, grevillea and bottlebrush) provide a great source of enrichment.

## IT IS IMPORTANT FOR YOU TO INTERACT WITH YOUR COCKATIEL.

• • • • • • • • •

## MAINTENANCE

Wash, rinse and refresh your cockatiel's food and water bowls every day. Regularly check and clean branches and toys to remove any poo. Replace the newspaper or shell grit in the bottom tray every few days. Don't forget to use a bird-safe disinfectant when cleaning. Worm your cockatiel every three months by placing a worming solution in their drinking water.

It is important for you to interact with your cockatiel. Your bird needs to spend plenty of time outside their enclosure exercising every day under supervision. A bird stand or play gym is a great way to provide your birdie with fun play time. You can toilet train your cockatiel or teach it to stay on its play gym so that it does not poo around the house or chew on something it shouldn't.

## DIET

Feed your cockatiel a fresh, varied diet every day. Your bird needs a cockatiel maintenance pellet and fresh vegetables and fruits (carrot, corn, beans, peas, spinach and apple). Millet sprays and unsalted nuts can also be offered as a treat once or twice a week. Seed mixes containing sunflower seed are very high in fat and should also only be offered to your cockatiel in small amounts as a treat.

Cuttlebone or a bowl of shell grit for calcium and vitamin D3 supplements in their drinking water a few times each week are also beneficial.

## CHECKLIST

- BIRD ENCLOSURE
- NATURAL BRANCHES AND PERCHES
- SHELL GRIT OR NEWSPAPER
- FOOD AND WATER BOWLS
- TOYS
- CAGE COVER
- BIRD STAND OR PLAY GYM
- FOOD
- WORMING SOLUTION
- BIRD-SAFE DISINFECTANT
- CALCIUM AND VITAMIN D3 SUPPLEMENTS

**BEN'S TOP TIP**

NEVER feed your cockatiel avocado, onion, apple seeds or chocolate as these foods can make them very sick.

**FUN FACT**

Cockatiels are the smallest member of the cockatoo family. They are closely related to the much larger sulphur-crested cockatoos.

# CHICKENS

**BREEDS:** ISA Brown,
Pekin and silkie

................................................

**LIFESPAN:** 8–10 years

................................................

**SIZE:** 2–3 kg

................................................

**MAINTENANCE LEVEL:** High

................................................

**COST:** $$

Chickens make great family pets. Chickens are also 'kind' on the environment. By eating food scraps, chickens reduce household waste and their poop makes fantastic fertiliser for the garden. Small breeds of chickens like Pekins and silkies are very cuddly and docile.

## HOUSING

House your chickens in an outdoor chicken coop or run. You need to consider how much space you have available and how many chickens you wish to keep when choosing the style and size of your coop. Your chickens need a sheltered area to roost and an open area to access fresh air and sunlight. Their coop must also be secure to prevent predators such as cats and foxes from getting in and to stop wild rodents from eating your chickens' food.

## EQUIPMENT

Your chickens will need food and water dispensers that should be placed off the ground on raised bricks or hung from the roof of the coop to help keep them clean. Secure perches inside the sheltered area for your chickens to roost on at night. Provide laying boxes with soft bedding (wood shavings or straw) for their comfort.

> **BY EATING FOOD SCRAPS, CHICKENS REDUCE HOUSEHOLD WASTE AND THEIR POOP MAKES FANTASTIC FERTILISER FOR THE GARDEN.**

## MAINTENANCE

Wash, rinse and refresh your chickens' food and water bowls every day. Regularly check and clean their perches and laying boxes to remove any poo. Completely replace the bedding in their laying boxes every 4 weeks. Don't forget to use a bird-safe disinfectant when cleaning. Use a chicken-safe insecticide to prevent mite and lice infestations. Worm your chickens every three months by placing a worming solution in their drinking water.

Chickens love having dust baths and scratching around in the garden looking for insects. Try to let your chickens out of their coop for a few hours each day to enjoy these activities, but only if they are safe from predators. Never forget to put them back in their coop in the afternoon. Your chickens will reward you for all your hard work with delicious, fresh eggs, so don't forget to take a basket.

151

# DIET

If you want to keep your chickens happy, healthy and producing plenty of eggs, you will need to provide them with a varied diet. Feed young chickens on a chick starter or pullet grower mix until they begin laying eggs. Once they start laying, a layer pellet should always be available to them.

A small bowl of scratch mix, fresh fruits and vegetables and household food scraps should also be offered daily. Provide shell grit or finely crushed eggshells for a great source of calcium to help your chickens produce eggs with hard shells.

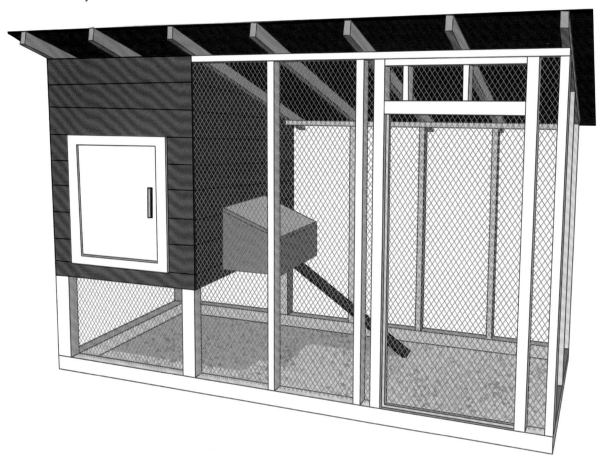

# CHECKLIST

- CHICKEN COOP OR RUN
- FOOD AND WATER DISPENSERS
- ROOSTING PERCHES
- LAYING BOXES
- BEDDING
- FOOD
- WORMING SOLUTION
- INSECTICIDE
- SHELL GRIT OR CRUSHED EGGSHELLS
- EGG COLLECTING BASKET

## BEN'S TOP TIP

Many councils will not allow you to keep roosters (your neighbours probably wouldn't be very happy with the early morning wake-up calls either). When sourcing your chickens, make sure they are all hens.

## FUN FACT

A laying hen can produce more than 300 eggs per year. Now that's a lot of omelettes!

# FINCHES

**SPECIES:** Zebra finch and star finch

**LIFESPAN:** 8–10 years

**SIZE:** 10 cm

**MAINTENANCE LEVEL:** Low

**COST:** $$

Finches make great feathered pets, particularly if you don't have the time to dedicate to interacting with a budgie or cockatiel every day. Watching your finches weave their nests is fascinating. What's most exciting is that finches will often breed in your aviary if you provide them with nesting boxes.

## HOUSING

An aviary provides the perfect enclosure for housing finches. When choosing an aviary, you need to consider how much space you have available and how many finches you wish to keep together. Smaller patio aviaries on wheels are perfect for one or two pairs of finches and groups of finches can be housed in a larger outdoor aviary.

Finches are highly social and should be kept in pairs or small flocks. More than one species may be housed together if the enclosure is large enough. Patio aviaries can be positioned on a sheltered verandah or inside your home. Outdoor aviaries must have a roof to provide shelter and plenty of shade so your birds don't overheat in hot weather.

**FINCHES ARE HIGHLY SOCIAL AND SHOULD BE KEPT IN PAIRS OR SMALL FLOCKS.**

## EQUIPMENT

Your finches need natural branches of different thicknesses throughout their aviary to perch on. Food and water bowls are essential. Seed dispensers can also be used to reduce food wastage. Finches love to bathe, so make sure you give them a shallow bath, especially on warmer days. Put shell grit or newspaper on the bottom of smaller patio aviaries and use wood chips or mulch as the base of outdoor aviaries.

Provide your finches with bunches of dry grasses to use as nesting material. Fresh native grasses and eucalyptus, grevillea and bottlebrush branches will enrich their environment. Don't forget the nesting boxes if you would like to breed your finches.

155

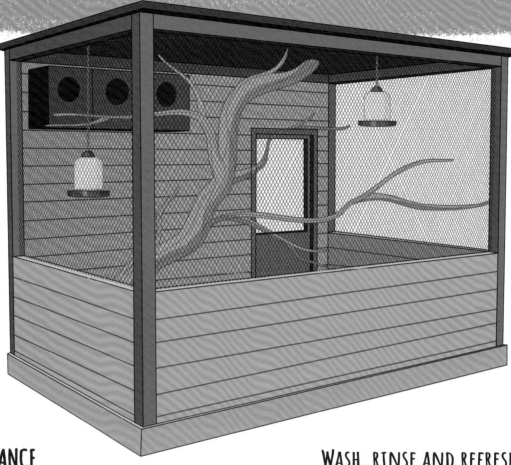

## MAINTENANCE

Wash, rinse and refresh your finches' food and water bowls every day. Regularly check and clean branches and nesting boxes to remove any poo. Replace the newspaper or shell grit at the bottom of smaller finch aviaries a few times each week. The base of outdoor aviaries should be replaced every month. Use a bird-safe insecticide to prevent mite and mice infestations. Don't forget to worm your finches every three months using a worming solution in their drinking water.

### WASH, RINSE AND REFRESH YOUR FINCHES' FOOD AND WATER BOWLS EVERY DAY.

## DIET

Feed your finches on a high-quality finch seed mix. They will also enjoy fresh leafy greens. Offer millet sprays and shell grit a few times each week. Add a vitamin supplement to their drinking water, especially if your finches are breeding.

—FEATHERED PETS—

## CHECKLIST

- PATIO OR OUTDOOR AVIARY
- NATURAL PERCHES
- FOOD AND WATER BOWLS
- SHALLOW BATH
- FOOD
- NESTING BOXES
- DRY GRASSES
- WORMING SOLUTION
- VITAMIN SUPPLEMENT

## BEN'S TOP TIP

Finches are lightning fast. Always take great care when opening your finch aviary so they don't dart past you and fly straight out the door.

## FUN FACT

Zebra finches' beaks change colour as they grow. Baby zebra finches have black beaks which change to orange and later red as they mature.

157

# QUAIL

**SPECIES:** Japanese quail

**LIFESPAN:** 4–6 years

**SIZE:** 100–120 g

**MAINTENANCE LEVEL:** Medium

**COST:** $$

Love the idea of caring for chickens and collecting eggs, but don't have a very large backyard? Perhaps Japanese quail might be the right pet for you. They are hardy and easy to handle, they don't take up much space and they lay gorgeous little speckled eggs.

## HOUSING

Use a rabbit hutch measuring at least 120 x 50 x 40 cm high to house one male and two female Japanese quail. Quail don't roost on perches like chickens, so most chicken coops do not make suitable quail enclosures. Never keep male quail (great rhyme!) together because they usually fight.

Your quail need a sheltered area to rest and feel safe and an open area to access fresh air and sunlight. Make sure their hutch is secure to prevent predators such as cats and foxes from getting in and to stop wild rodents from eating their food.

## EQUIPMENT

Place food and water dispensers on raised bricks or hang them from the roof of your hutch to help keep them clean. Japanese quail are great egg layers, so make your quail comfortable by putting wood shavings or straw to lay in inside their sheltered area.

## JAPANESE QUAIL ARE EASYGOING BIRDS THAT TOLERATE SMALL AMOUNTS OF GENTLE HANDLING.

· · · · · · · · · · · · · · · · · · · ·

## MAINTENANCE

Wash, rinse and refresh your quails' food and water bowls every day. Regularly check and clean their sheltered area and laying boxes to remove any poo. Completely replace their bedding every week. Don't forget to use a bird-safe disinfectant when cleaning. Worm your quail every three months by placing a worming solution in their drinking water.

Japanese quail are easygoing birds that tolerate small amounts of gentle handling. You can even take your quail for a walk in the backyard if you watch over them. Never leave your quail out alone as they may not return to their hutch like chickens usually do.

## DIET

Feed young quail on a chick starter crumble until they begin laying eggs. Once your quail start laying they should be fed on a poultry layer mash or crumble. Chicken pellets are often too course for quail to swallow and are not suitable.

Your quail should also be fed fresh fruits and vegetables every day. Offer a scratch mix, some seeds and even live insects as treats a few times a week. Provide shell grit or finely crushed eggshells for a great source of calcium.

**YOUR QUAIL SHOULD ALSO BE FED FRESH FRUITS AND VEGETABLES EVERY DAY.**

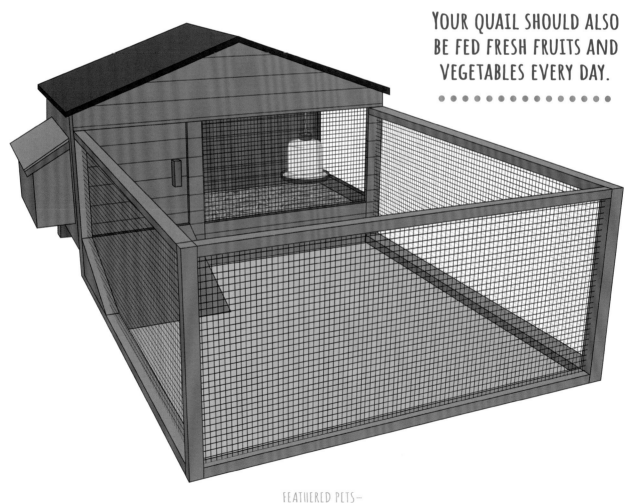

## CHECKLIST

- RABBIT HUTCH
- FOOD AND WATER DISPENSERS
- BEDDING
- FOOD
- TREATS
- SHELL GRIT
- WORMING SOLUTION

### BEN'S TOP TIP
Quail enjoy dust baths. Place a tray of dried dirt inside their enclosure a few times each week for them to scratch in. They will love it!

### FUN FACT
Japanese quail eggs have been incubated and hatched in space. This makes quail the first birds in space.

—PET BUDGET—

# PET BUDGET

TYPE OF PET

## SET UP COSTS

COST/ADOPTION FEE OF ANIMAL    $

HOUSING & EQUIPMENT

$

$

$

$

$

$

$

$

$

$

**SET UP TOTAL**    **$**

## ONGOING COSTS

FOOD

$

$

$

MAINTENANCE

$

$

$

VET CARE    $

**ONGOING COSTS TOTAL (Yearly)**    **$**

Photocopy and complete this template each time you're considering a new pet

# PET PROPOSAL

**PREFERRED PET**

**LIFESPAN**

..............................................................................................................................................

**SPACE NEEDED**
How much room does your pet need?
Where will your pet be housed at your home?

..............................................................................................................................................

**DIET**
What does your pet eat?
Where will you buy your pet's food from?

..............................................................................................................................................

Photocopy and complete this template each time you're considering a new pet

164

## CARE REQUIRED

When will you look after your pet? (before/after school)
How long will it take each day/week?

..............................................................................................................

## COST OF CARE

Attach your completed Pet Budget.

..............................................................................................................

## CONCERNS

Address any concerns the adults in your life may have about you getting
this pet. Use the tips in the 'Convincing the adults' section in this book.

..............................................................................................................

Photocopy and complete this template each time you're considering a new pet

# *Pet Pledge*

I _____ commit to loving and caring for my pet,

_____ always.

I promise to do my very best to meet my animal's needs in every way
I possibly can, to live our best lives together.

Insert photo of you with your pet

I also pledge to be an animal ambassador for all creatures
and the precious environment we all depend on.

Signed: _____

Witness: _____     Date: _____

Photocopy and complete this template each time you're considering a new pet

# PET DICTIONARY

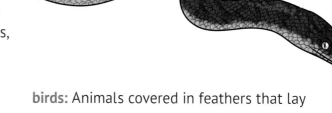

**alternative pets:** An animal not typically considered a traditional pet.

**amphibians:** Vertebrates that often begin life in the water with gills and then develop lungs and live on land as adults (such as frogs, toads, salamanders, newts and caecilians).

**aquatic:** An animal that lives in water.

**arachnids:** Invertebrates with eight legs (such as spiders and scorpions).

**arboreal:** An animal that climbs or spends much of its time in a tree.

**basking:** When an animal sits in the sun to increase its body temperature.

**bio culture:** Good bacteria that can be added to an aquarium to help keep the tank clean.

**birds:** Animals covered in feathers that lay eggs, have a beak and wings and typically fly.

**breed:** A group of animals, within a species, that have been developed by humans for a purpose. It also means when animals mate to produce babies.

**calicivirus:** A deadly disease in rabbits spread by wild rabbits, mosquitoes and other insects.

**carnivore:** An animal that only eats other animals.

**communal:** A group of animals that live together.

**compost:** Broken down organic material that can be used as a fertiliser for plants.

**crepuscular:** An animal that is most active during the early mornings and evenings.

**dander:** Tiny flecks of shed skin.

**diurnal:** An animal that is most active during the day.

**domestication:** The process of taming an animal or changing it over time for human purposes.

**draught:** A current of cold air blowing through a room.

**dry dock:** A land area for a semi-aquatic animal such as a turtle to climb onto.

**ectotherms:** Animals that rely on the environment to generate heat and regulate their body temperature.

**ethical:** High standards of animal welfare.

**endotherms:** Animals that generate their own heat to regulate their body temperature.

**enrichment:** Improving or enhancing an animal's life through stimulation.

**exoskeleton:** A hard covering on the outside of the body of some invertebrates.

**feline:** A cat or other member of the cat family.

**fish:** Invertebrates with fins that live solely in water.

**fluorescent:** Bright, tube-shaped lights.

**fry:** Baby fish.

**hatchling:** A young animal that has recently emerged from an egg.

**herbivore:** An animal that only eats plants.

**humidity:** Moisture levels in the air of an animal's enclosure.

**hygrometer:** A device used to tell the humidity inside an enclosure.

**hypoallergenic:** An animal less likely to cause an allergic reaction.

**impulse pet purchase:** Purchasing a pet without any planning or research.

**insects:** Invertebrates with six legs such as crickets, cockroaches and bees.

**insectivore:** An animal that feeds on insects.

**interactive pet:** A pet that needs lots of hands-on attention.

**invertebrate:** An animal without a backbone (such as insects, spiders and scorpions).

**juvenile:** A young animal.

**life cycle:** The different stages of an organism's life.

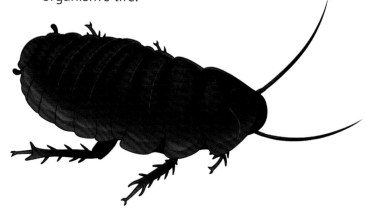

**mammals:** Warm-blooded animals that have fur, give birth to live young and feed their young on milk.

**morphing:** Changing from one thing into another (the tadpole morphed into a frog).

**moult:** When an animal sheds old feathers, hair or skin to make way for new growth.

**nocturnal:** An animal that is most active during the night.

**observational pet:** A pet that should not be handled, as it may cause stress or injury to the animal.

**omnivore:** An animal that eats both plants and animals.

**oxytocin:** A feel-good hormone released in your body when you stroke animals.

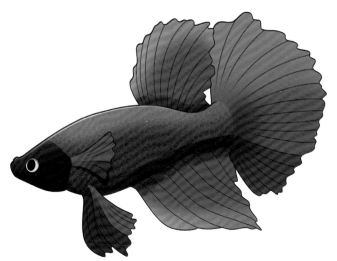

171

**organic:** Something that has come from living matter.

**parthenogenesis:** Refers to animals that can reproduce without male fertilisation (such as stick insects).

**pH:** A number that describes the acidity or alkalinity of water.

**phasmids:** Insects with long legs that look like sticks or leaves.

**predators:** Animals that naturally prey on others.

**reproduce:** Create babies.

**reptiles:** Vertebrates mostly covered in scales (such as snakes, lizards, crocodiles, turtles and tortoises).

**rodents:** Mammals that love to chew and have constantly growing incisor teeth (such as mice and rats).

**sentient:** Refers to creatures that have emotions and can think and have feelings, like us.

**shed:** The process of removing old skin to make way for new skin underneath.

**siphon:** A tube or hose used to drain water from a tank.

**solitary:** An animal that lives on its own.

**stimulation:** Encouraging an animal to become more active and display natural behaviours.

**substrate:** Bedding or material placed on the floor of an animal's enclosure.

172

**supplement:** A vitamin or mineral added to an animal's diet to make it more nutritious.

**terrestrial:** An animal that lives on land.

**thermal gradient:** A change in temperature over distance.

**ultraviolet light (UV):** Radiation given off by the sun that is important for the healthy growth and development of many animals.

**vaccinations:** Treatment with a vaccine to produce immunity against a disease.

**vertebrate:** An animal with a backbone (such as mammals, reptiles, birds, amphibians and fish).

**zoonotic disease:** A disease that can be transmitted from animals to people.

First published in 2022 by New Holland Publishers Sydney
Level 1, 178 Fox Valley Road, Wahroonga, NSW 2076, Australia
newhollandpublishers.com

A record of this book is held at the National Library of Australia.

ISBN: 9781760792114
Group Managing Director: Fiona Schultz
Project Editor: Liz Hardy
Designer: Ana Heraud
Production Director: Arlene Gippert
Printed in China

10 9 8 7 6 5 4 3 2 1

Keep up with New Holland Publishers:

[f] NewHollandPublishers

[o] @newhollandpublishers

[o] Follow Ben's animal adventures
@bendessen as well as www.bendessen.com.au